<mark>Projects for Parents</mark>

Rainy Day Projects for Children

Gerri Jenny
Sherrie Gould

Murdoch Books
Nazareth, Pennsylvania

Dedications:	With love and gratitude to my mother, Christine Waite Covert, my first and best teacher. *Gerri Jenny* In loving memory of my sister, Katherine McFarland Pitzer. *Sherrie McFarland Gould*
Project Editor:	Mary Ruth Murdoch
Cover Design:	Joe Ragont, Joe Ragont Studios
Photography:	Jim Whitmer, Photographer Mary Whitmer, Creative Director Kitty Wilson, Production Assistant
Models:	Jill Lederhouse, Jamelyn Lederhouse, Joshua Evans, Bethany Gibbons, Karen Taylor, Lauren Taylor, Lindsey Taylor, Ryan Taylor, Mark Howard, Annika Whitaker, Nicholas Perry, Bobby Gulley, Erin McCallum
Illustration:	Roland Bruce Macdonald
Project Testing:	Eleanor Murdoch (age 5 1/2), Sarah Murdoch (age 3 1/2)
Special Thanks:	Joseph Allegretti, JoAnna Bennett, Jim Brand, Bryce Craig, Del Kahn, John Laser, Michele Kyriss, Mike and Carol Powills, Charles Silvey, and Cliff Stieglitz.
Address all inquiries to:	Murdoch Books, Inc. P.O. Box 390 Nazareth, PA 18064

ISBN: 1-878767-61-5

1 2 3 4 5 6 7 8 9 **96 95 94 93 92 91 90**

Manufactured in the United States of America

CONTENTS

LET'S BEGIN

The man seated next to me at the college graduation ceremony was quietly, unashamedly, making a spectacle of himself. He could not take his eyes off a young woman. Enthusiastically, he waved, blew kisses, winked, smiled, and mouthed, "I love you," all the while flashing photographs at high speed!

The young woman, it turned out, was his daughter, "Julie." She was no raving beauty, but she'd been named Homecoming Queen and "Woman of the Year." She was an athlete, a scholar—an all-around success.

How does a plain-looking preschooler grow up to be a queen? Simple. Julie had an encouraging father who believed in spending time building up his children. His confidence in her in turn gave Julie the ability to believe in herself. This young woman developed the self-esteem necessary to succeed in scholastics, sports, and relationships with schoolmates.

Our purpose with this book is to help you spend time developing a nurturing relationship with your child. This is more than a series of projects—we hope that you will spend the time you invest in these projects building a loving, caring, supportive relationship with your child.

About this book:

The projects presented on the following pages cater to a wide range of capabilities. Some of these projects will require more parental participation than others. As with any activity, you should use your judgment in selecting projects to try—older children will need little guidance with several of the projects, and other projects may be a little beyond the reach of younger boys and girls. In some instances we've included suggestions for simplifying projects where it might be appropriate.

At the end of each project we've included some suggestions for activities or conversations to have with your son or daughter. By talking as you work on the project together, you'll build a stronger relationship.

The materials used in the projects generally are inexpensive and easy to obtain. The Basics chapter that follows gives you a list of materials to start with. We've tried to use many products you already have in your home. Of course, you can mix and match the parts of the different activities. Feel free to experiment!

Many of the projects require parts to be cut or holes to be punched. Please remember these safety rules as you work:

Use the proper tool for each job—don't try to make a pair of scissors do the work of a utility knife. If particular tools are required (scissors, etc.) we will indicate them at the beginning of each project.

If you're using a utility knife (they're very handy!) don't use a dull blade to cut with—any carpenter will tell you that you end up pushing or cutting harder with a dull blade, and therefore run a greater risk of slipping and getting a deep cut. Use a sharp knife, but please, do NOT let your child handle sharp implements.

Before you begin any project, read the entire set of instructions and consider carefully whether you can make the craft safely with the tools you have. If you have any doubts, stop. Take the opportunity to talk with your child about the importance of working safely, and go to the hardware store for the right tool. That's a lot cheaper than a trip to the emergency room.

Look through the projects in the book, and see which ones strike your fancy. Check off the items you'll need from the Basics chapter and head for the hobby shop. When you come home, make the Rainy Day Fun Box project first—it will be the perfect place to keep all your project goodies. Armed with this Rainy Day Fun Box, common household items, and a child, you'll have lots of fun and rewarding times. We have!

Gerri Jenny and Sherrie Gould

A word of caution:

THE BASICS

A few of the things you'll need—crepe paper, craft glue, pompoms, felt, construction paper, pipe cleaners, and a utility knife.

Some of the projects in this book require something special—a toothpaste box, a handful of walnuts, or wooden mixing spoons. But most of the projects require simple household items and the materials shown on the list below.

Pack the items into a special craft box that you can store under a bed. When there's "nothing to play with" you can pull out your craft box and make something special with your child.

Try this: make a duplicate of your craft box, and send it to Grandma's house. Small children get bored easily when the grownups want to talk, so having a craft box already there will give them something fun and educational to do.

THINGS YOU NEED:

Construction paper, all colors, large and small sized sheets

Clear and colored contact paper

Crepe paper

Tracing paper (you can use typing paper, if you have it)

Posterboard, a few pieces in basic colors

Crayons and markers

Pencils, lead and colored (for older children)

Craft glue that bonds well to cloth and other materials

Household glue—used for paper projects

Dry powder tempera paint (it is inexpensive and easy to mix)

Cookie cutters in animal and seasonal shapes

Safety scissors

Utility knife (sometimes called a "Stanley®" knife)

Magnet tape

Clothespins, spring and non-spring types

Wooden doll stands (available at craft or hobby shops)

Pompoms (get 1/4", 1/2", 1", and 2" sizes)

Felt, all colors

Paper fasteners (or "brads")

Pipe cleaners

Popsicle sticks

Stickers—stars, animals, and other designs

Other decorative trim—braid, rickrack, yarn, wiggle eyes, etc.

Depending on where you shop, you can expect to pay around $35 for all the Basics. We've found that hobby or craft stores have most of the items—but you can find many of the Basics in your grocery store. Make a project of getting all the bits and pieces with your child! He'll find the hobby shop a fascinating place, and he'll want to jump right in to your first project when you get home.

LET'S CHAT:

PERFECT
PROJECTS

"But there's nothing to do . . ."

How many times have you heard that phrase uttered by a child standing amidst a roomful of toys? Haven't you found it extremely frustrating?

When your child was born she was completely dependent. Everything she ate, wore, or played with was brought to her. Even if it doesn't seem that way, your child has made great progress in the past few years in learning to act on her own.

The child knows that there are things to play with. But she is probably tired of making choices and is really asking you to tell her what to do. Adults are used to starting projects or activities by themselves, but young children sometimes need direction and encouragement.

These projects are perfect for those moments—when you need to say, "Let's make . . . ." As you work together, encourage your child to make some small decisions by herself. Have her pick colors or sizes, or choose which rocks will be Pebble People or Pebble Pets. If she's not willing to make choices—fine. Tell her which rocks to paint purple, which to paint green, and so on. Have an enjoyable time working together!

The projects in this section will appeal to children of all ages. The Autumn Wreath was perfect for Lauren, a three-year-old who came to our photo session with her mom. Young children can practice their painting and gluing skills with the Pebble People and Pets. The Rainy Day Fun Box makes a perfect place to store all of your project materials. The Countdown Chain makes a perfect project for the child who just can't wait for a birthday, Christmas, or some other event.

Older children will enjoy Door Decorations. They can make special items to decorate their own doors or the doors of other family members. All of the projects provide you with the opportunity to spend precious time with your children.

Have fun!

RAINY DAY FUN BOX

A practical project for starters! Decorate a box for holding all your basic project supplies. Together, decide on an alliterated name for the box such as Adam's Awesome Box, Bonnie's Beautiful Box, Carol's Creative Box, Dan's Designer Box, etc.

THINGS YOU NEED:

Large sweater storage box (the long, low shape is great for easy accessibility and storage under the bed)

Construction paper

Glue

Scissors

Photograph of your child

Crayons, markers

Glitter

Magazine pictures (optional)

- Glue your child's photograph on a large construction paper design of your choice; then glue the design to the box lid.

- Print the name you have chosen on the box. If your child does not write yet, use a crayon to make a dot-to-dot of the chosen box name for him to trace the dots. Imagine his sense of accomplishment when he says, "I did it myself!"

- Decorate the box with cut-out designs representing some hobbies and interests of your child. Pictures can be drawn, cut, and pasted onto the box. Use magazine cut-outs if you wish. Both of you will be using this box for a long time to come. Make it as attractive as possible!

LET'S CHAT:

What special things does your child like to do? This box can hold supplies for lots of project ideas! Which projects should you do first?

AUTUMN WREATH

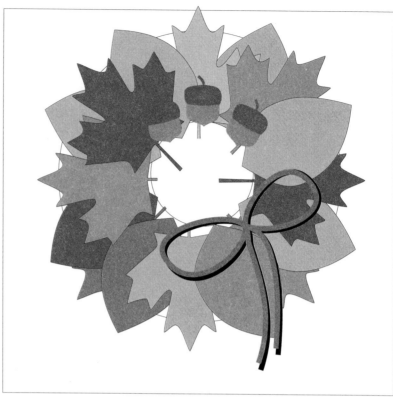

This project can be wonderful for older children, but it also makes an excellent first project for a very grown up three-year-old. Put on your hats and raincoats, and go collect the ingredients. Have some hot cocoa when you get back, and start right in!

THINGS YOU NEED:

Colorful leaves, nuts, and tiny pine cones

Paper plates

Glue

Ribbon

Scissors

Pencil

LET'S BEGIN:

- Lay a glass or cup upside down on the paper plate. Trace around the glass, and cut out the circle, leaving a doughnut shape.

- If you've collected wet leaves, let them dry. If your child is impatient, you can put them in the oven on a cookie sheet. CAUTION: Leaves will singe or burn in a hot oven. Be safe: don't set the oven for more than 250 degrees.

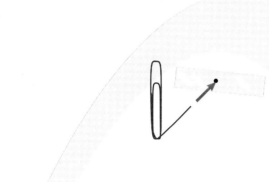

Push the paper clip through a piece of tape. The tape reinforces the paper plate, so it won't tear.

- Glue the leaves onto the plate first. Then put nuts and pine cones in place.

- Tie a ribbon bow and glue it on. Let the project dry.

- Put a piece of tape on the back of the paper plate at the top of the wreath. Poke a hole through the plate (and the tape reinforcement) with a paperclip, and hang up the wreath.

You can make paper plate wreathes at other times of the year. At Christmas, for instance, cut small squares of old wrapping paper and glue them on for a collage effect. Colorful tissue paper squares fluffed out make a unique wreath too!

Ask your child what his favorite season is and why he likes that time of year the best.

LET'S CHAT:

COUNTDOWN CHAIN

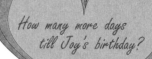

In every child's life there are times when waiting for a special event or holiday is just too hard! This Countdown Chain will enable your child to visualize exactly how many more days it is until a vacation, birthday, Grandma's visit, Easter, or Christmas. With a Countdown Chain he won't be pestering you all the time with questions of "How many more days?"

THINGS YOU NEED:

Construction paper

Scissors

Glue

Stickers

Markers

LET'S BEGIN:

• You will make a link for each day until the Big Event. Cut construction paper into strips, 1" wide by 6" long, but make the last strip longer than the others (1" by 9").

• Form a loop with one strip; glue. Insert one strip inside the other, and glue. Continue in this way until all but the top link has been added. For the last link, make the loop but leave an extended strip sticking out.

Some patterns to
use for your
Countdown Chain . . .

- Glue a picture or design appropriate to the Big Event onto the extended strip. (For example, use a sun for a trip to the beach, a child's photo for an upcoming birthday, or a star for the days until Christmas.)

- Make small designs to glue on each link—fish for a beach trip, candles for the child's birthday or Christmas—and number each one. On the side of each link, glue a numbered shape, starting with the largest number at the bottom of the chain.

- 10, 9, 8, 7, 6, 5, 4, 3, 2, 1 . . . You're ready for a great time anticipating the future with this Countdown Chain!

LET'S CHAT:

If you have more than one child, you may find that you spend a lot of time talking about patience with the child who *doesn't* have a birthday coming. A small child is still developing his sense of time and may not have grasped the idea that he will have a birthday someday, too. Enlist his help. Would he like to be in charge of making the Door Decorations (see page 24)? Would he like to think of presents to give to his brother or sister?

PEBBLE PEOPLE AND PETS

Rocks become pretty pets or peculiar people. Let your imaginations run free in what you can create from stones with a few simple touches. Look for forms and faces in rocks. When you combine them with other odds and ends, you may not have a lofty work of art, but you will have FUN!

THINGS YOU NEED:

Rocks of various shapes and sizes
Markers
Craft glue
Felt
Wiggle eyes, pipe cleaners
Tempera paint

LET'S BEGIN:

• Wash and dry the rocks. Study each rock to see whether it has the potential to be a Pebble Pet or a Pebble Person.

• Paint a design on each rock with tempera paint.

• Apply felt features and wiggle eyes to the rocks, and glue the rocks together.

• Be sure to cut a piece of felt for the bottom of the rock. (This will prevent the rock scratching another surface.)

• Your Pebble People projects make perfect paper weights!

LET'S GIGGLE:

Try saying that last sentence two or three times. . . .

PLACEMATS & NAPKIN RINGS

Making placemats and napkin rings is an easy project that doesn't require a lot of preparation. It's also a perfect project if you have more than one child—younger children can color their placemats while older children use scissors, paste, and glue.

Napkin Rings

THINGS YOU NEED:

Scissors

Glue

Paper towel, wrapping paper, or toilet paper tubes

Contact paper or wallpaper (ideal; if you have extra kitchen wallpaper make matching placemats and napkin rings)

Markers or crayons

Stickers

LET'S BEGIN:

- Cut the tubes into 2" sections. Make one for each family member.

- Cut the contact paper (or wallpaper) into 2" strips and glue a strip to each napkin ring.

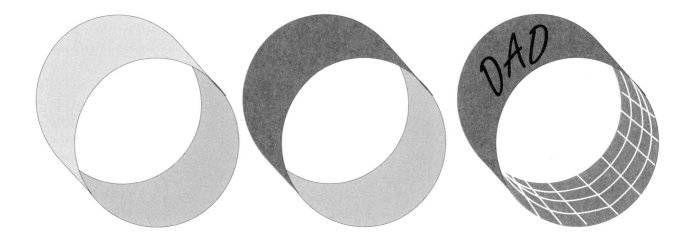

- Letter each family member's initials onto felt or construction paper. Then cut and glue the initials onto the rings.

- You can also decorate the napkin rings with stickers, markers, or designs cut from felt or contact paper.

Placemats

THINGS YOU NEED:

Photographs, magazine pictures, or wallpaper

Scissors

Glue

Cardboard, posterboard, or construction paper

Clear contact paper

Markers or crayons

Stickers

LET'S BEGIN:

- Cut the cardboard, posterboard, or construction paper into 12" by 14" rectangles. Make one for each family member.

- Cut a 12" by 14" rectangle of wallpaper and glue it to the placemat. Or arrange photographs or magazine pictures to

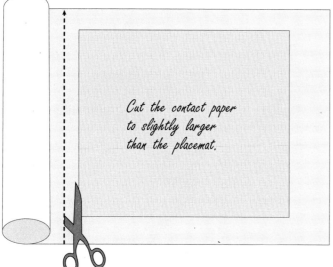

Cut the contact paper to slightly larger than the placemat.

Carefully peel back a small part of the contact paper backing . . .

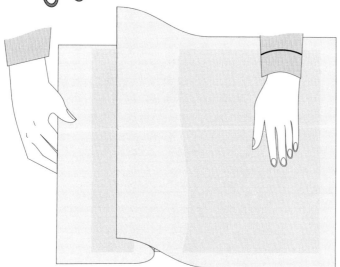

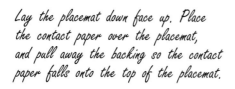

Lay the placemat down face up. Place the contact paper over the placemat, and pull away the backing so the contact paper falls onto the top of the placemat.

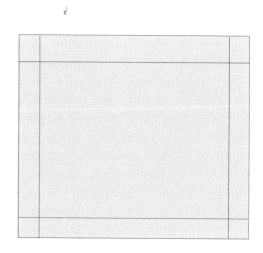

Turn the placemat over, and fold the extra contact paper over onto the back.

Cut a second piece of contact paper slightly smaller than the placemat, and place it on the back.

make a collage. Try to use photos of each person and pictures that mean something special (hobbies, etc.).

- You may want to decorate each placemat with stickers, construction paper shapes, or drawings to match the napkin rings.

- Cover each placemat with clear contact paper cut to size. It's a good idea to cover both sides of the placemat: overlap the contact paper onto the back side of the placemat by about 1/2", then cover the back (see illustrations). The slightest bit of moisture or grease on the table will make construction paper become discolored.

- Now each family member has a matching set—a placemat and napkin ring lovingly handcrafted by your joint efforts!

This would be a good opportunity to teach your child about how to set a table properly: "Let's use the new placemats and practice where to put the napkin, fork, knife, spoon, glass," etc.

LET'S CHAT:

SPONGE FLOWERS

These flowers are awfully cute, and they can be practical, too. A child will love the animal or letter shapes and can use them for sponge painting or educational games. Our junior project tester used her *S* to "clean" the bathroom sink, the kitchen counters, the children's play table, the cat. . . .

THINGS YOU NEED:

Small household sponges

Green pipe cleaners

Glue

Masking tape

Scissors

Construction paper

Baby food jar

Contact paper

LET'S BEGIN:

• Using scissors, cut the sponges into different shapes, numbers, and letters.

Bend a pipe cleaner in half and twist the ends together. Press the top of the loop down to the twisted ends, forming

two leaves. Twist the leaves together with a straight pipe cleaner "stem."

- Insert the flower stem into the sponge to form the flower. Make a bouquet of flowers by repeating the process.

- Cover a baby food or mustard jar with contact paper to make a decorative vase.

- Sponge Flowers are great for sponge painting activities. Remove the sponges, dip them in tempera paint, and apply them to sheets of construction paper. After dipping the sponges in fabric paint, you can decorate t-shirts and sweat shirts!

Play educational games using the flowers. Ask, "What shape is this?" "What number am I holding?" "Can you spell out your name with the sponge letters?"

LET'S CHAT:

DOOR DECORA-TIONS

Put yourself in your child's place for a minute. You've had a tough day at school—the teacher is drilling you on multiplication tables—and you're beat. You come home, go up to your room, and discover the Three Bears on your door! Door decorations are a fun way to surprise each other or other family members. Included here are several ideas that are appropriate for holidays, birthdays, and seasonal celebrations. Conspire with your son or daughter to decorate a door today!

To ensure that your projects will be reusable, apply masking tape strips to the back of your project. Roll up small tape pieces in donut shapes and press them on the strips to hang. This will save wear and tear on your artwork!

Birthday Child

Birthdays are very special days. A great way to begin the day is with a special Birthday Child door decoration! Try to match some of your child's favorite clothes with construction paper— if your son likes red, use red paper!

Construction paper

Scissors

Glue

Yarn and ribbon (optional)

String

Glitter

Markers

Masking tape

Tracing paper

LET'S BEGIN:

- Cut balloon shapes in three colors of construction paper. Knot a 12″ string around the bottom nub of each one.

- Write "Happy Birthday _____"—one word on each balloon—in glue. Sprinkle glitter on top and let the glue dry. Shake off any excess glitter. (Hint: put the glitter in a salt shaker and shake it on.)

- Trace the boy or girl pattern pieces onto tracing paper. Cut the pieces out and use them as patterns for cutting the construction paper. Glue the construction paper pieces together to make your boy or girl.

- Cut out and glue on the facial features (see illustration). Draw the shoes with markers, or use the patterns shown.

- Draw on hair with markers or cut, curl, and glue paper strips. Or make yarn hair; for example, cut small yarn strands and glue them on the head for a boy. For a girl, cut twelve strands of yarn 3′ long and knot all the strands together. Divide the hair into three sections of four strands each; make one braid and knot the end. Tie ribbon bows on each end, and glue the braided hair on the girl's head as shown. Use your imagination to create a close approximation of the way your child wears his or her hair.

- Apply masking tape strips to the back of the child's body and press rolled-up pieces of tape to the strips. Mount the child's body on the bedroom door, and tape the balloon strings to the child's hand. Happy Birthday!

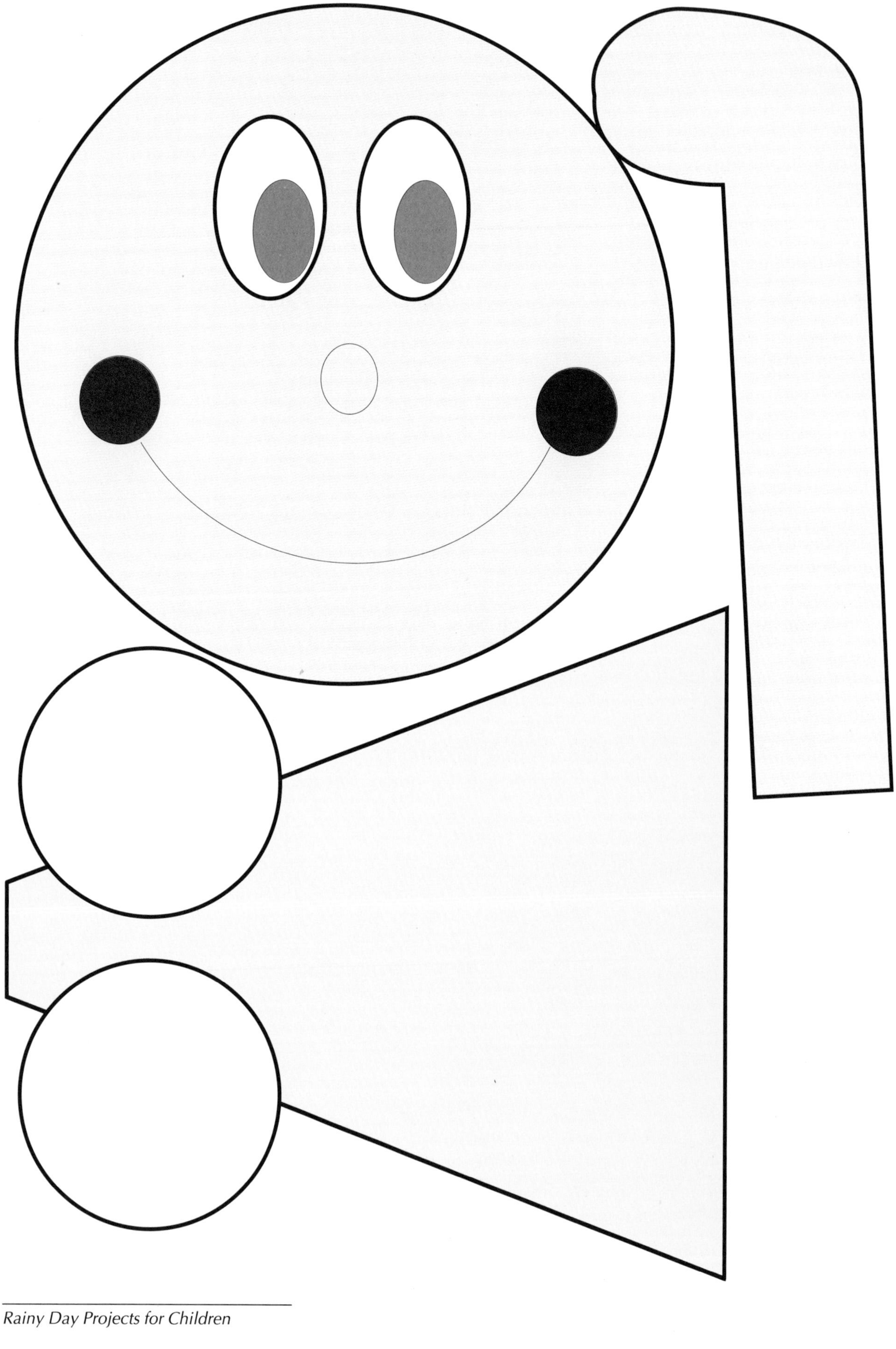

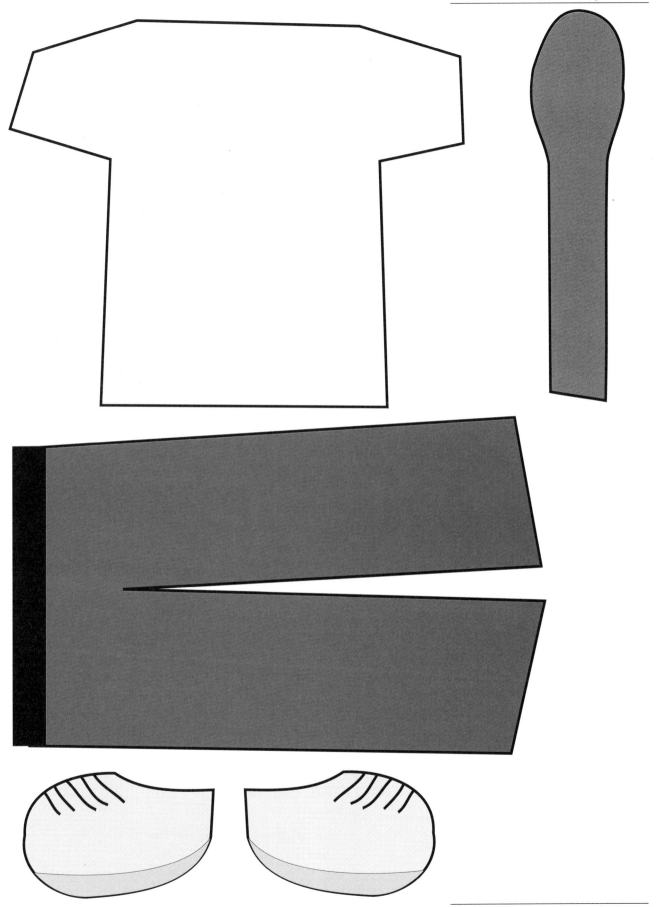

Baby Bear

The Three Bears all have similar shapes. Daddy Bear and Mommy Bear are just proportionally bigger than Baby Bear.

Trace and cut Baby Bear's parts. Then lay them on your fabric and cut an extra 2" around to make Mommy Bear.

Cut out Mommy Bear, lay her down on the fabric, leave a 2" "margin" and cut Daddy Bear.

LET'S CHAT:

Why not design a birthday person for mother, father, grandma or grandpa? Knock on their bedroom door and see their delighted reactions—not too early, however!

This can be a good project to do with a brother or sister. Many times younger boys and girls think "it's not fair that Annie gets to have a birthday, but I don't!" Talk with your child about birthdays, and whether your child's birthday will ever come. For a particularly impatient child, you might make the Countdown Chain on page 14.

Storybook Door

The Three Bears are favorite storybook characters of many children. We have chosen them for our Storybook Door, but use your imagination: What are some of your child's favorite storybook characters? Can you make them into a Storybook Door that will delight your child?

If you want to make the three bears, you might get some fake fur at the fabric store. Your bears will last much longer and have a more three-dimensional appearance.

Construction paper

Scissors

Glue

Masking tape

Fake fur (optional)

Markers

Tracing paper

LET'S BEGIN:

- Copy the bear patterns onto tracing paper. Cut them out, and use them as patterns for cutting the construction paper (or fabric).

- Cut the eyes and bear muzzles from construction paper. Draw a nose and mouth on each muzzle with markers, then glue facial features onto the bear heads. Add eyelashes to Mama Bear (cut and fray black paper as eyelash fringe).

- Apply masking tape strips to the backs of the bears and press rolled-up pieces of tape to the strips. Mount the Three Bears on the doors.

LET'S CHAT:

Read *Goldilocks and the Three Bears* together. Ask your child what part of the story he likes the best. You might include a lesson on the importance of not talking to strangers! What mistakes did Goldilocks make? How can we learn from our mistakes and the mishaps of others?

BOXES AND TOYS

It's a gray and rainy day outside. Your children have cabin fever, and the forecast is for four more days of the same miserable weather. You're about to lose your mind. What do you do?

Make an airplane! Make puppets! Have fun! Each of the projects in this section requires simple household items, plus a few goodies from your Rainy Day Fun Box. You can turn ordinary household boxes and containers into houses, schools, caterpillars, airplanes, and bears and discover a lot of new ideas for storing your children's toys.

While making these projects, underscore to your children the idea that you are being creative with the things you have—instead of wishing for something else. You probably shouldn't try the "when I was your age I had to . . ." routine, but it can be important to show children the value of being self-reliant.

You needn't stress the character-building aspects of these projects—do them because they're fun! As your child works through the projects—playing, discovering, and inventing—he is also learning to be self-sufficient. And he probably doesn't even realize it.

As we said above, the projects in this section don't require much beyond the Basics materials listed on page 6. Very young children will enjoy making the Crayon Kangaroo (especially if you have to make cupcakes to empty the liner box!). The Giraffe, Spaghetti Caterpillar, Cockatoo, and Cuplet Puppet projects will interest older children—they can be much more involved in shaping what the finished project looks like.

Most of the projects in this book should take between forty-five minutes and two hours to complete. The Fun City Project will take much longer. It includes smaller sub-projects for making houses, landscapes, schools, slides, trees, signs, and people; you and your child can work on this for a long time. It's a perfect activity if you have a child home from school sick for several days. It's also a great idea if you've traveled to Grandma's for a visit, but the weather keeps the children indoors for a week.

TOOTH-PASTE AIRPLANE

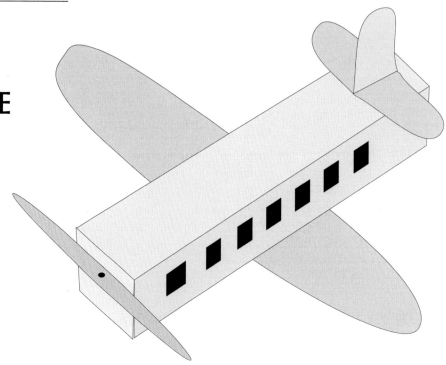

The best toys encourage your child's imagination and sense of creativity. In this project you'll help your youngster as she makes an airplane from a toothpaste box. This exciting toy will hold your little pilot's attention long after the propeller's first spin—and help keep her teeth clean!

The box dimensions shown in the artwork are for a Crest® 6.5 oz. tube. Other toothpaste boxes are similar, but you may have to adjust the measurements.

THINGS YOU NEED:

Construction paper

Toothpaste box

Paper fastener

White household glue (Elmer's® Glue, for instance)

Black marker

Scissors

Tracing paper

LET'S BEGIN:

• Hold your toothpaste box against the pattern shown. Check to be sure your box will fit the pattern. If it doesn't, you have to make some adjustments as you go along.

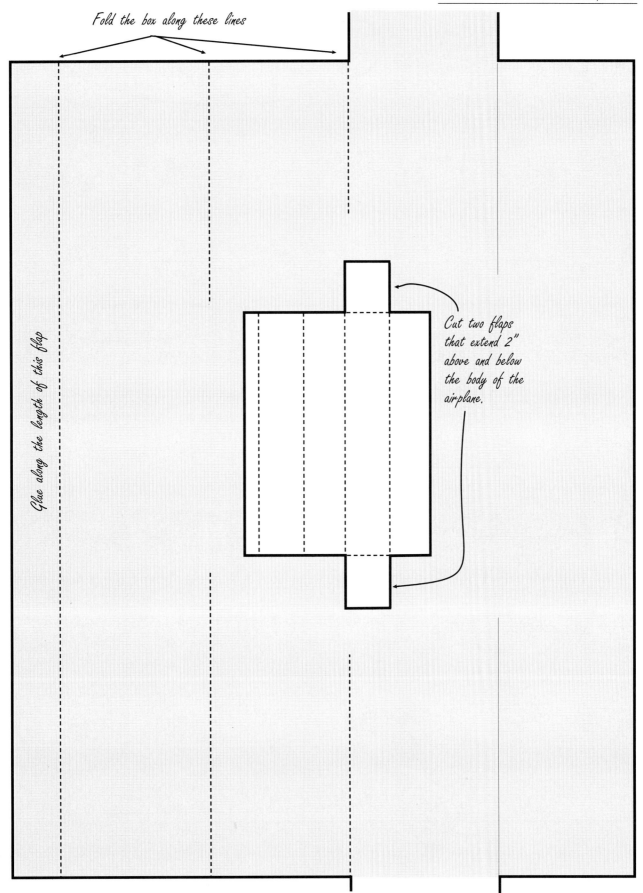

Fold the box along these lines

Glue along the length of this flap

Cut two flaps that extend 2" above and below the body of the airplane.

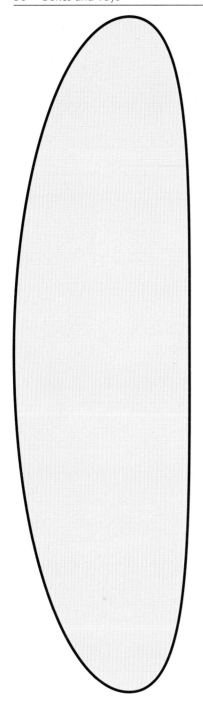

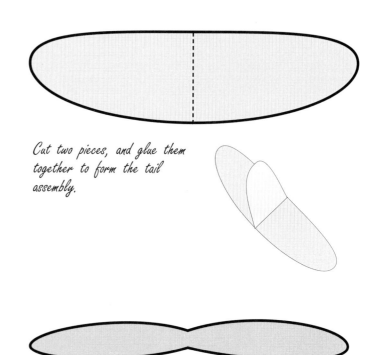

Cut two pieces, and glue them together to form the tail assembly.

- Trace the body, wings, propeller, and tail patterns onto tracing paper. Cut out the pieces and use them as a guide to cut the construction paper.

- Open the top of the toothpaste box. Run a bead of glue from the top of the lid along the back side of the box, and place the box down on the airplane body.

- Glue the rest of the airplane body to the box.

- Glue the wings and the tail on the airplane as shown.

- Attach the propeller to the box lid with the paper fastener.

- Use a black marker to draw in the airplane windows. Now you are ready to fly away!

LET'S CHAT:

Having a toothpaste airplane is fun! But will you let your child carry a tube of toothpaste throughout the house (if it gets lost, how will her teeth get brushed tonight)? When pilots fly airplanes, they have to be very careful about putting everything just where it belongs. Agree with your child that the toothpaste airplane belongs in the bathroom; even if it flies somewhere else to visit, it has to land in the bathroom at the end of the trip.

CONSTRUC-TION PAPER BEAR

Here is a "bear-ry" good place to store a great deal of construction paper for future artistic endeavors!

THINGS YOU NEED:

3.4 lb. laundry detergent box
Contact and construction paper
Markers
Glue
Tracing paper
Scissors

LET'S BEGIN:

- Carefully cut the top off the detergent box. Once that's finished, take a damp paper towel and wipe out the inside. (You don't want leftover soap on your construction paper.)

- Cover the detergent box with construction paper.

- We've included a variety of bear fashion accessories—the bow can be a bowtie for boy bears or a lovely hair bow for girl bears. You can decorate your bear with a necktie, "bear-et," or cap. Copy the bear parts onto tracing paper.

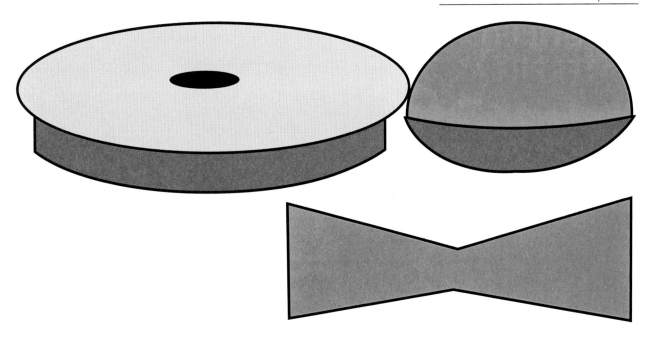

Cut the pieces out and use them as patterns for cutting construction paper.

- Glue the bear parts onto the box as shown. Color in the eyes, nose, ears, and paws.

- Fill your bear with paper!

If you have more than one child, you might want to make a Construction Paper Bear for each. (Theoretically they'll spend less time squabbling over which construction paper belongs to whom.)

LET'S CHAT:

Your Construction Paper Bear is big and sturdy. Where is a good place to keep him? Talk with your child about keeping the crayons, chalk, and other related items in the same place. Can you make another project that would help do the trick? (You might try the Crayon Kangaroo project on page 51.)

SPAGHETTI CATERPILLAR

This colorful caterpillar will hold hair ribbons, long toys, or art supplies. You may want to create him just for a toy!

You can make this project with a full box of spaghetti just as easily as with an empty box. If you use a full box, your next project can be making a spaghetti supper!

THINGS YOU NEED:

Spaghetti box (1 lb.)

Construction paper

Glue

Scissors

Markers

Tracing paper

LET'S BEGIN:

- Cut six 2" by 8" strips of different colors of construction paper. Glue them in bands across the box as shown.

- Trace the caterpillar head, antennae, and foot patterns onto tracing paper. Cut the pieces out, and use them as patterns to cut the head, antennae, and six feet from various colors of construction paper.

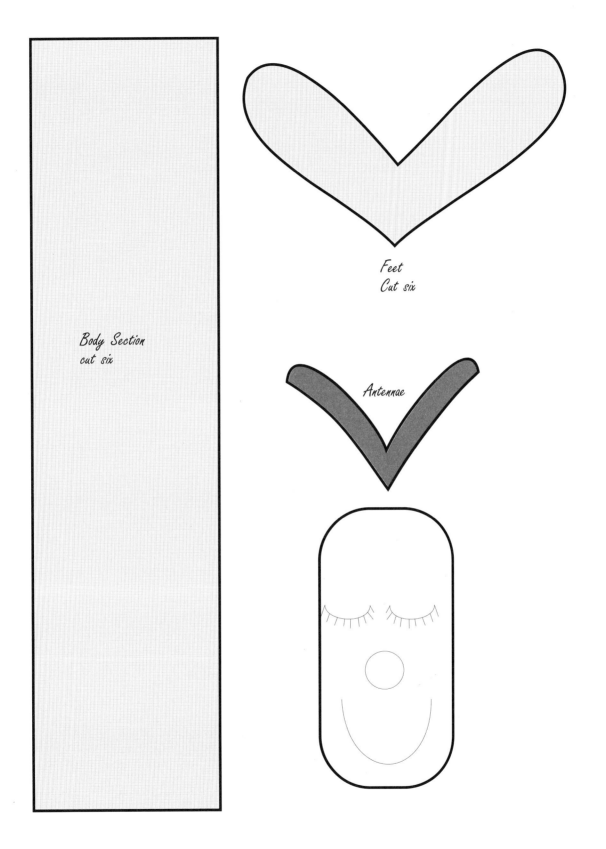

Feet
Cut six

Body Section
cut six

Antennae

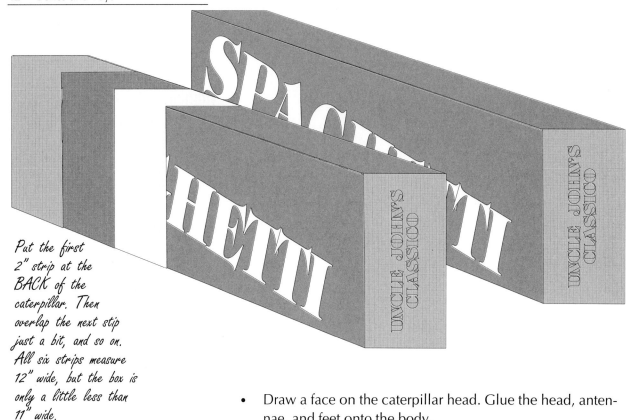

Put the first 2" strip at the BACK of the caterpillar. Then overlap the next stip just a bit, and so on. All six strips measure 12" wide, but the box is only a little less than 11" wide.

- Draw a face on the caterpillar head. Glue the head, antennae, and feet onto the body.

- Done! Isn't he cute enough to cuddle?

LET'S CHAT:

God made caterpillars in a special way—they become butterflies! Your caterpillar won't become a butterfly, but it could turn into spaghetti for supper. . . .

COCKATOO

Real cockatoos come from Australia and the South Pacific, of course, but this cockatoo comes from a pasta or cereal box. This colorful project is a very good choice for little hands that are learning to use scissors and glue, but older children will enjoy being able to do most of the project by themselves.

THINGS YOU NEED:

Cereal or macaroni box

Construction paper

Glue

Scissors

Markers

Tracing paper

LET'S BEGIN:

- Cut the box diagonally as shown, and cover the two pieces with construction paper.

- Glue the two triangles together in a bird shape, as shown in the diagram.

- Trace the feet, beak, wing, and tail feather patterns onto tracing paper. Cut out the pieces and use them as patterns

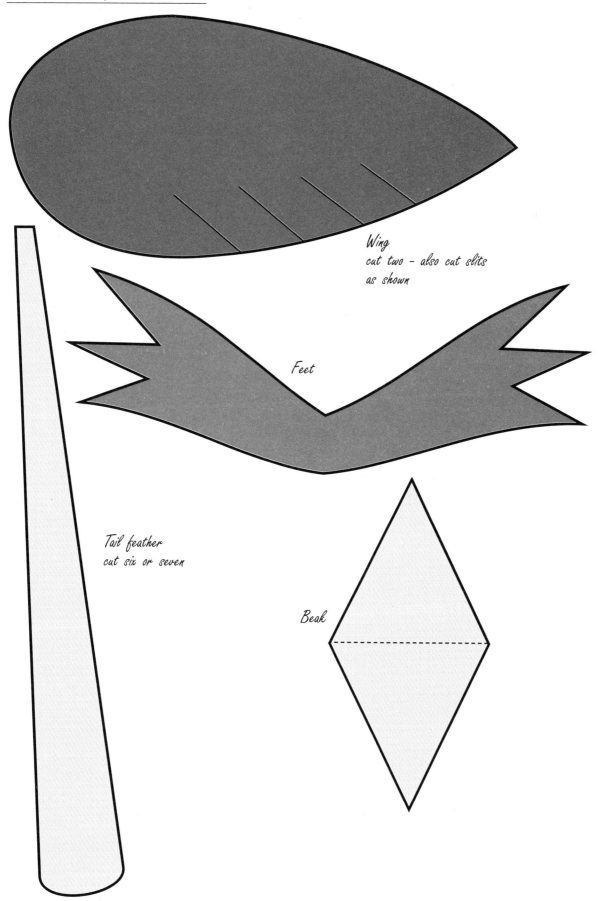

Wing
cut two – also cut slits
as shown

Feet

Tail feather
cut six or seven

Beak

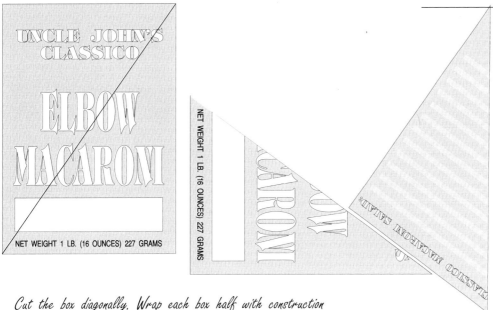

Cut the box diagonally. Wrap each box half with construction paper, and glue them together as shown.

to cut the construction paper. Remember to cut two wings and six colored feathers. Glue them on the cockatoo as shown.

• Draw on the bird's eyes. Does he look like a cockatoo to you?

What kind of bird is a cockatoo? Where does a cockatoo live? Cockatoos live in the South Pacific, but they also live at the zoo. If you wanted to see a cockatoo, how far would you have to travel?

LET'S CHAT:

CUPLET PUPPET

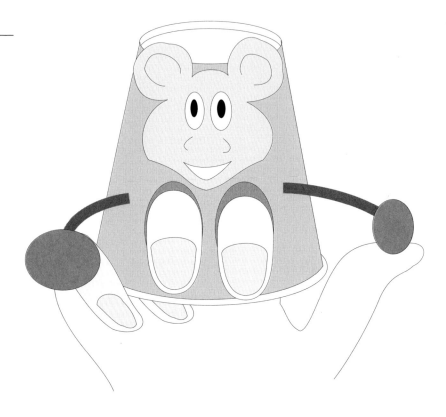

Let your fingers do the walking and provide all the action needed for this Cuplet Puppet. This can be lots of fun for children of any age, and they don't take long to make.

THINGS YOU NEED:

Paper cups

Construction paper

Pipe cleaners

Yarn or felt

Scissors

Glue

Markers or crayons

Tracing paper

LET'S BEGIN:

- The grownup should use a pair of sharp, pointed scissors to cut two small finger holes at the bottom edge of the cup. Do *not* let the child do it.

- Copy the designs onto tracing paper. Cut the pieces out, and use them as patterns for cutting construction paper. Glue the parts onto the cup as shown.

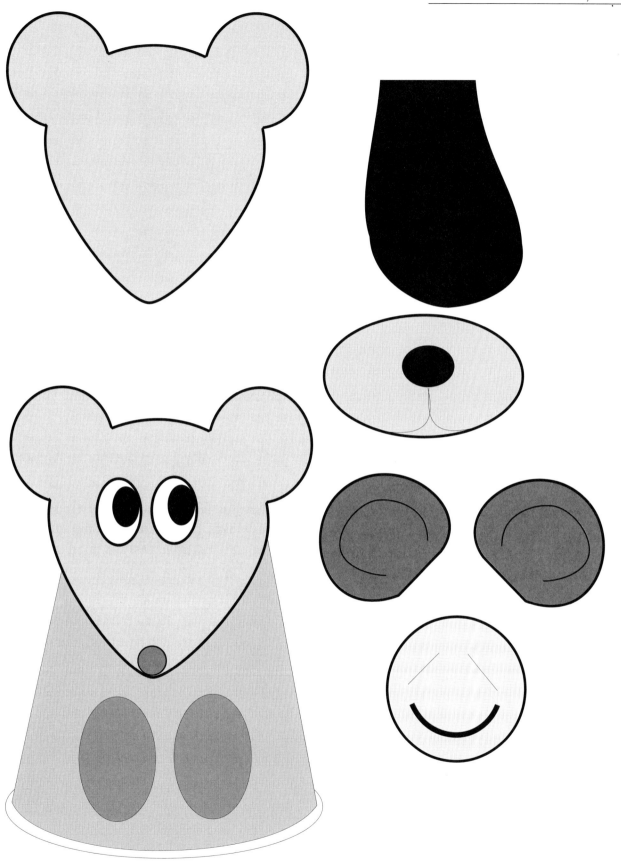

- Make facial decorations from scraps of yarn or felt. You can simplify the project by using crayons instead.

- Push pipe cleaners into the cup to make arms, a tail, or hair.

- Depending on where you position the holes, your child's fingers can be arms or legs. Cut 1" strips of construction paper and loop them around your child's fingers to make pants or shirt sleeves.

- Make several puppets so they can walk, run, jump, hop, and talk to each other!

LET'S CHAT:

Paper cups are an essential part of every picnic basket. Discuss with your child where you would like to go on your next picnic. Backyard picnics are fun, too!

GIRAFFE

Rear view

The long neck of the giraffe makes him a perfect choice to hide your rulers, markers, and pencils!

THINGS YOU NEED:

Pringle's® potato chip can

Construction paper

Glue

Scissors

Contact paper (optional)

Tracing paper

LET'S BEGIN:

- Cover the can with contact or construction paper. Trace the giraffe parts onto tracing paper. Cut the pieces out, and use them as patterns for cutting the construction paper.

- Draw the giraffe's face on with markers. Glue the body parts on the can as shown in the diagram.

- Cut paper "spots," and glue them on the giraffe. If you have a hole punch, you can mass produce spots quickly.

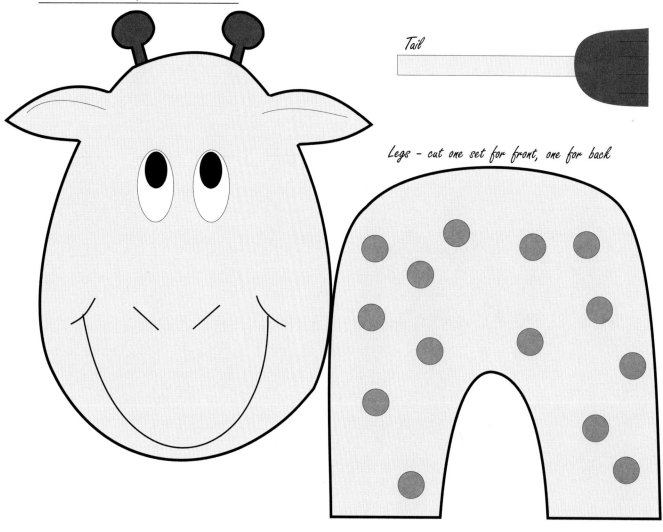

Tail

Legs - cut one set for front, one for back

LET'S CHAT:

When she was a little girl, Gerri was nicknamed "Geraldine the Giraffe," and hated it. Her oldest son had a special nickname when he was very little—until the day she yelled it loudly at a Little League game. Does your child have nicknames he or she has outgrown?

CRAYON KANGAROO (OR TULIP)

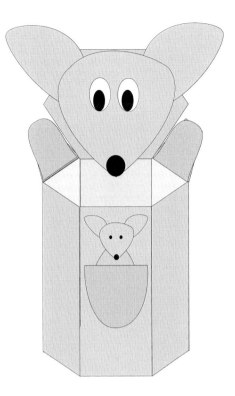

Use a cupcake liner box to make crayon containers! If you have two children who fight over crayons, these containers can help solve the problem. Of course, now they may fight over who gets which box!

THINGS YOU NEED:

Paper Maid® Bake Cups cupcake liner box

Contact paper

Crayons or markers

Scissors

Construction paper

Glue

Tracing paper

LET'S BEGIN:

- Cover the outside of the box and both sides of the lid with brown contact paper. Remember: you must be able to open and close the lid when you're done.

- Copy the baby kangaroo and the kangaroo face, pouch, and paw patterns onto tracing paper. Cut the pieces out, and use them as patterns for cutting the construction paper. If you can, use two shades of brown paper: lighter

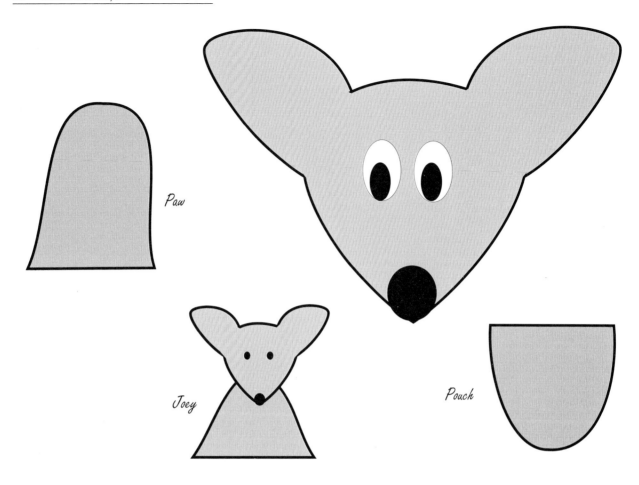

Paw

Joey

Pouch

for the large kangaroo face and darker for her paws and pouch and the baby.

- Glue the kangaroo face to the inside of the box lid. With a crayon or marker, draw the eyes and nose on the face. Glue the kangaroo's front paws to the two small flaps. Draw lines on the kangaroo's paws to highlight the toes.

- Glue the baby and the pouch to the outside of the box as shown. Now you have a new crayon box!

Here's an alternate suggestion:

- The patterns also show variations for a tulip project. Cover the outside of the box (but not the lid) with green contact paper.

- Copy the patterns for the tulip flower and leaves (the kangaroo paws) onto tracing paper. Cut out the pieces and use

(Use the paw pattern for the small leaves)

them as patterns to cut two tulips and two leaves from construction paper.

• Glue a flower to each side of the lid and the leaves to the two small flaps. The Tulip Crayon Box is now ready to blossom with crayons!

Did you know that a baby kangaroo is called a "joey"? Do you know why? Plan a trip to your local library and see if you can find the answer!

Discuss the value of neatness with your child. Why is it important to organize supplies and toys? What are the benefits of having everything in its place and easy to locate?

LET'S CHAT:

TREASURE CHEST

Every child needs a place to keep his special treasures, those "prizes" that are valuable only to him. Gerri's teenage son still has a seahorse that they found together at the seashore many years ago. Your child can store his or her treasures in this very special box.

THINGS YOU NEED:

Cigar box or box with lid

Contact or wrapping paper

Felt

Ribbon

Glue

LET'S BEGIN:

• Cover the box with contact or wrapping paper, making sure that the lid opens easily.

• Decorate the outside of the Treasure Chest to suit your tastes. You could use special feathers, nuts, stones, or pine cones that you two have discovered.

• Line the inside bottom of the box with felt.

Glue the ribbon or string to the box on the bottom, at the front and back.

- Glue the ribbon onto the bottom of the box, at the front and back. Tie the ribbon into a big bow on top of the box to keep it closed!

This special box is for storing your child's valuables, but "value" is a pretty abstract concept to a child. What are the most valuable things we have? What are your child's most favorite things? How valuable are Mom and Dad? Be sure to tell your child how valuable he or she is to you!

LET'S CHAT:

FUN CITY

Design a portable city all your own that will be used as a backdrop for numerous happy hours of play. Give this fantasy city a name and decide what you wish to include in it . . . a pond, bridge, houses, streets, people, trees, or shrubbery.

This project, done completely, will take a lot longer than two hours. It's ideal for a child who is sick or trapped inside for a long spell of miserable weather.

Town and Buildings

THINGS YOU NEED:

Posterboard

Dairy cartons—different shapes and sizes

Construction and contact paper

Scissors

Aluminum foil

Craft glue

Markers

Tape

LET'S BEGIN:

- Tape two pieces of posterboard together to make a large playing board. Cut the streets from construction paper and glue them onto the posterboard (you might use a Matchbox® car to measure the road width). Be sure to draw the stripes in the middle of each road!

- Pull the tops of the cartons apart, and cover them with contact paper to depict houses, stores, a school, the post office—whatever buildings you want in your city.

- Cut windows, doors, and the roof of contrasting colored contact or construction paper, and glue or press them in place.

- Use markers to draw on building features such as door windows, curtains, and doorknobs. Print building names on their fronts. Insert toothpick flags in the school, library, and post office buildings.

Long Pond

School

The Office

Tape two pieces of posterboard together, and lay out your version of Fun City. If your little city planner gets tired of one version, cover the posterboard with construction paper and start over!

My House!

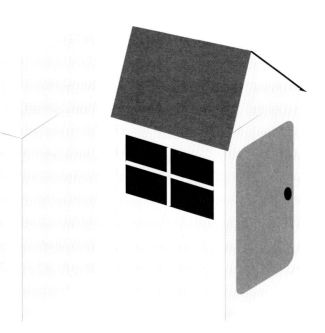

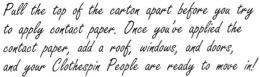

Pull the top of the carton apart before you try to apply contact paper. Once you've applied the contact paper, add a roof, windows, and doors, and your Clothespin People are ready to move in!

- You can decorate dwellings and buildings with flowers and colorful accents using markers or crayons.

- Make a replica of your own home. (Quart milk cartons are great for taller buildings.) Use the same color door, shutters, and bricks that are on your dwelling. Don't forget to add your street number!

When architects or planners conceive of a project, they frequently make very detailed models of what the finished building or development will look like. What would it be like to build a real version of Fun City? Would your son or daughter like to do that?

LET'S CHAT:

Clothespin People

Who are the people that live in Fun City? You can use clothespins to make a variety of people. Artists and caricaturists rarely show all the details when they draw a person—instead they highlight a few recognizable elements of the subject's appearance. Do the same thing with your people—does your child have relatives who are bald? Wear glasses? Think of ways to make your Clothespin People look like people in your neighborhood!

THINGS YOU NEED:

Non-spring clothespins

Felt and material scraps

Decorative trim—braid, rickrack

Two or three cotton balls, or scraps of yarn

1/4" pompoms

Fine tip markers

Craft glue

Tempera paint

Wooden doll stands (available at craft stores)

Scissors

Paintbrush

Pipe cleaners

Sand paper (optional)

- Sand the clothespins to remove any roughness. This is an important step before painting.

- Look at the characters shown in the diagrams for ideas. Which characters will you make?

- What clothes will they wear? Paint the trousers and doll stands with tempera paint on each character who will wear pants; let them dry.

- Will your Clothespin People have hair or hats? For hair, squeeze some glue onto a piece of paper. Grasp some strands of yarn in your fingers tightly and "stipple" the ends in the glue. You should have the ends of the yarn fairly saturated with glue when you attach them to the tops of the Clothespin People's heads. Let the glue dry.

- Use cotton balls for grandmothers; pull the cotton balls apart until the fibers are loose and easily shaped. Glue the fibers to the head as above. Let the glue dry.

- For hats, cut a 1/2" circle from felt; glue this to the top of the Clothespin People who will wear hats, then glue a 1/4" pompom on top of the felt.

LET'S BEGIN:

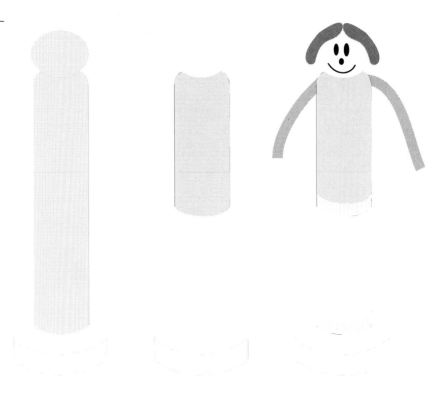

- Use fine tip markers to draw on facial features and glasses, a mustache, or other distinguishing features.

- Cut pieces of felt or material to 1 1/2″ by 2 1/4″. Wrap them around the top half of the clothespin to make a shirt, jacket, blouse, or dress bodice; glue. Braid or rickrack glued down the front or the back can serve as buttons. Cut skirts from felt or material, or use a strip of wide lace.

- Cut a number of pipe cleaners in half—glue one on the back of each character's neck as arms. Then insert each clothespin person in a doll stand.

LET'S CHAT:

Talk with your child about the people you've made. Why did you make them? Do they look like people in your neighborhood? Would your child like to show them to the people they represent?

Decorations

What is a city without trees, bushes, signs, and play equipment? What will the people do?

When your child was just a baby, he only perceived a world that was a few feet around him. As he has aged, the "world" he sees has gotten larger. Do you permit him to cross the street yet? Making the various parts that decorate Fun City may very well expand your child's view of where he lives. All of a sudden street signs, buildings, playgrounds, and other such things will take on a new meaning, and your child's horizons will be broadened.

Strips of posterboard or cardboard

Construction paper

Aluminum foil

Yarn

Tracing paper

Scissors

Glue

Hole punch (optional)

THINGS YOU NEED:

Swing set
Place this pattern on the edge of a folded
piece of posterboard. The top of the slide
should be on the fold.

Cut signposts from
construction paper.
Fold the post in half,
and staple at the fold.

Cut the slide from a piece of posterboard. Color in the steps with a marker, and cover the slide with aluminum foil.

Trees and Shrubs:

- Cut strips of posterboard or cardboard to various lengths and widths for tree trunks and shrubs.

- Fold and staple the strips at the top as shown. By spreading the unstapled ends, you can make your trees and shrubs stand up.

- Cut the green tree tops and shrubs from construction paper and glue one to each of the strips.

Street Signs and Stoplights:

- Cut and letter street and road name signs in appropriate shapes and colors.

- Cut stoplights in a rectangular shape. Cut small circles of red, yellow, and green, and glue them on. If you have a hole punch, punch circles from construction paper and glue them in place.

- Cut strips of cardboard in various lengths and widths for sign poles. Fold and staple the strips at the top as shown; the signs and stoplights will stand up when you spread the unstapled ends. Glue the signs and stoplights to the folded strips.

- Be sure to make a sign with your own street name!

Swing and Slide:

- Trace the swing and slide patterns onto tracing paper. Cut the pieces out and use them as patterns for cutting the construction paper.

- Cover the slide with aluminum foil and fold it along the fold lines shown in the illustration. Draw squares as slide steps with black marker.

- The cardboard or posterboard swing frame will look like a capital H. Fold the cardboard or posterboard in half, and lay the pattern down along the fold. Cut along the pattern.

- Tape the swing seat to the middle of a strand of yarn. Tape the yarn ends at the top underneath the folded swing frame.

Set up your city scene, using small toy cars on the roads. Make a country area outside the city if you have a big board. Cut out a pond or lake and glue it on. Why not add little animals? (Either make them or use small toys.) Add more features to your ever-changing city in future project sessions!

LET'S CHAT:

Discuss the colors and shapes of stop, yield, and other traffic signs with your child. Teach her this ditty:

"Always watch the traffic light when you skip and hop,
Green means go, yellow means slow, and red means STOP,
STOP, STOP!"

GIFTS
GALORE

"And I made it all by myself!"

Is there any sentence that a child can say with more excitement, enthusiasm, or pride? It's important to encourage your child to give presents to other people—your child should learn the value of expressing love for others. It may be difficult, especially with preschoolers, to convince your child that he has to give his Fuzzy Pencil Friends away. But learning the value and the joy of gift-giving is an important part of growing up.

In making a gift, a little of the child goes with it. The recipient will appreciate the thought, time, and energy that went into creating the present. When your child is complimented for his efforts, he can proudly say, "And I made it all by myself!" Imagine what that will do for his self-esteem!

The projects in this section are ways for a child to make a gift for someone he cares about. The projects are all inexpensive and easy to make. The youngest children will enjoy making the Bird Balls, and they'll be *very* helpful with the Brownie Basket. (You decorate the basket while they keep an eye on the brownies!) Preschoolers and primary-age children will have no trouble with the Magnetic Puzzles, Cookie Cannikin, or the Lovable Lollipops. From our experience as preschool and elementary teachers we think the Laced Cards make wonderful projects for teaching hand-eye coordination. The Bumblebee Note Holder and the Fuzzy Pencil Friends involve some gluing and will require an older child or more help from the grownup.

Many of the projects in this section turn out to be wonderful toys for your own children. Our two project testers made off with the original Lovable Lollipops, and they haven't been seen since. Even if you don't have any birthdays or gift-giving occasions coming up, think of a reason to make some of these projects today!

BIRD BALL

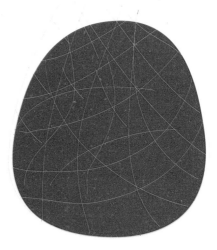

Birds and flying can fascinate a little child (or a grownup!). This project is perfect for the youngster who wants to do all the work himself—you can supervise as your child creates a special present for the birds in your neighborhood.

Remember, though, that birds make their nests in early spring—if you do this at other times of the year, birds may take quite a while to take the strings. The peanut butter and seeds ideas shown below will work anytime.

THINGS YOU NEED:

Plastic netting that vegetables come in
Twist ties
12" piece of heavy string
Yarn, thread, string strands

LET'S BEGIN:

- Put the yarn, thread, and string strands together in a loose ball inside the netting.

- Tightly close each end of the netting with a twist tie.

- Insert the heavy string through one hole in the netting and out another. Tie the ends of the string together.

- When the weather is nice, take a walk together and find a tree limb or bush on which to hang your Bird Ball. Try to choose a spot where your child will be able to watch the birds from a house window.

- Birds will gather the strands of yarn, thread, and string to build their nests.

Additional "Gifts for the Birds":

- Tie a string around a pine cone and suspend strands of yarn and heavy thread from the cone to offer the birds another nest-building gift.

- Tie a piece of yarn through a pine cone, then roll it in peanut butter and in bird seed. Suspend it from a tree branch or bush. Birds will light on the cone and peck at the seeds.

- Spread peanut butter on a piece of stale bread and sprinkle a variety of seeds on top. Use a straw to poke a hole through the bread top, insert a piece of yarn or string through, and hang it from a tree or bush.

Happy bird-watching!

LET'S CHAT:

Where do birds live? How do they make nests? Baby birds need nests to live in, just as little children need homes to live in. If it's lunchtime, a child might need a peanut butter sandwich (without the seeds).

BROWNIE BASKET

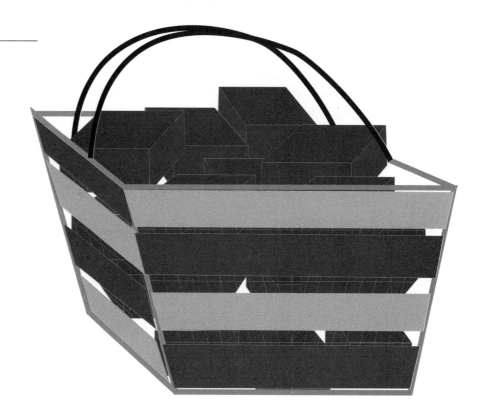

This attractive gift requires just a few materials and a little hand-eye coordination. It's a great project for a child to make "all by myself!" Once you've made the basket, make brownies together and take them to a friend.

THINGS YOU NEED:

Plastic berry basket
Two pipe cleaners
Ribbon
Felt or cloth

LET'S BEGIN:

- Weave the ribbon in and out through the basket holes along the sides. When the weaving is done, glue the ribbon end inside the basket.

- Cut the felt or cloth to the size of the basket bottom. Glue it in place and let it dry.

- Make a double handle for the basket by attaching each pipe cleaner to opposite sides of the basket. (For stability, the handles should be at least 1" apart.)

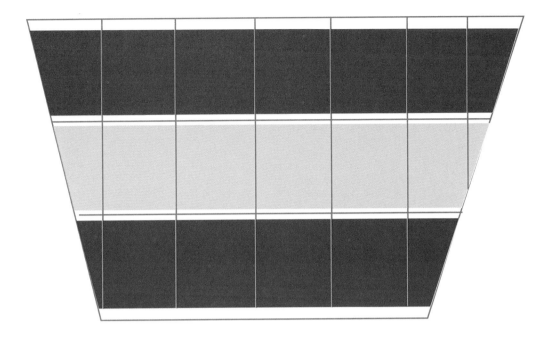

- Fill the basket with brownies or other tasty tidbits and take them to a friend!

LET'S CHAT:

When we give gifts to other people we are showing our love to them. Discuss with your child some other ways we can show our love to the people we care about.

COOKIE CANNIKIN

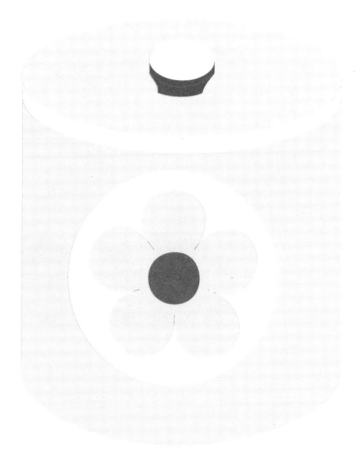

Banish rainy day blues by baking cookies or brownies together. Have further fun creating a "Cookie Cannikin" to hold your delicious goodies. The recipient will enjoy your tempting treats and then appreciate your decorative container for many days to come!

THINGS YOU NEED:

Coffee can with plastic lid

Contact paper

Scissors

Glue

Drawer knob with screw or shank button with pipe cleaner (optional)

Felt squares, cookie cutters, paper doily; rickrack or other decorative trim

Pencil

Black marker

- Cover the coffee can with contact paper.

- Decorate the lid with felt, paper doily, or contact paper designs.

- Trace some cookie cutters onto felt or contact paper. Cut out three or four shapes.

- Press or glue the shapes onto the can. Glue the rickrack or other decorative trim around the bottom edge. Let it dry.

- Fasten the knob (if you're using one) to the lid.

- Letter "COOKIES" on the lid with marker, if desired.

- Put some yummies in your tummies! (But save some for the cannikin!)

LET'S CHAT:

Making cookies and brownies is fun. But we have to eat good things, too, so that we can be healthy. Talk with your child about your rules for "junk food," how much is too much, and so forth. Stress how important good food is for growing children.

BUMBLEBEE CLOTHESPIN MAGNET

Refrigerator magnets are so practical and popular these days. You can make one together for clipping on your child's artwork or love notes for Grandma!

THINGS YOU NEED:

Small spring-type clothespin

Magnet tape

One 1" black pompom

One 1" yellow pompom

One 1/2" black pompom

Yellow or black felt

Yellow or black pipe cleaner

Tiny wiggle eyes

Small red felt scrap

Glue

LET'S BEGIN:

- Cut the pipe cleaner into two 1" lengths; bend and glue them to the top of the 1" yellow pompom so that the "antennae" will be just behind the head (the 1/2" black pompom).

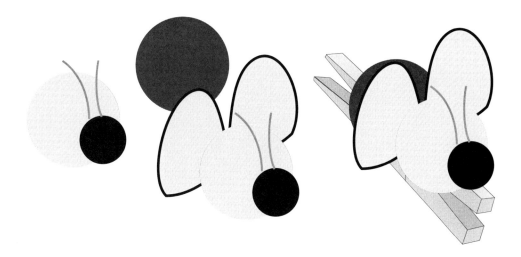

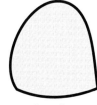

Actual size

- Glue the bee head (the 1/2″ black pompom) to the yellow pompom.

- Glue the wiggle eyes onto the head (small felt circle eyes can be substituted).

- Cut a small mouth of red felt, and glue it in place.

- Cut out the wings from yellow or black felt, and glue them onto the back of the yellow pompom.

- Glue the black 1″ pompom to the yellow pompom to complete the bee body. Glue all three pompoms to the top of the clothespin, and let the glue dry.

- Stick a small piece of magnet tape to the back of the clothespin.

- You can make the gift extra special by making your own note paper. Cut out small squares of paper and decorate them with marker designs. Insert the paper into the clothespin jaws for gift giving.

Your child is probably more used to getting gifts than giving them. When do you give gifts to people? Do you need a special occasion?

LET'S CHAT:

FUZZY PENCIL FRIENDS

These little creatures are simple to assemble—and a good way to spend a rainy afternoon with several children. If you have enough pieces (and pencils) you can have hours of fun. They will be great giveaways as children's party favors or just as surprises for special friends!

THINGS YOU NEED:

New unsharpened pencils
Craft glue
1/2" pompoms
Wiggle eyes
Felt

LET'S BEGIN:

- Glue the pompoms in a straight line near the pencil eraser. Let the glue dry.

- Glue the eyes to the last pompom facing the eraser. You can also tie a ribbon around the pencil, or cut a felt design and glue it onto the pencil before you put the pompoms on.

LET'S CHAT:

Our world has many kinds of "fuzzy friends" that move in a variety of ways. Discuss with your child the manner in which animals move. Which animals crawl on the ground? Fly in the sky? Swim in the water? Run on the land? Climb trees?

LACED CARDS

As former preschool teachers, we recommend making Laced Cards because they are excellent projects for developing eye-hand coordination. Children enjoy doing the lacing, and the cards are so attractive that they become permanent keepsakes!

THINGS YOU NEED:

Construction paper

Hole punch

Masking tape

Scissors

Long yarn strand

Facial tissue

LET'S BEGIN:

- Draw a large simple shape on a piece of construction paper. Place one piece of construction paper on top of another and cut the shape out of both pieces.

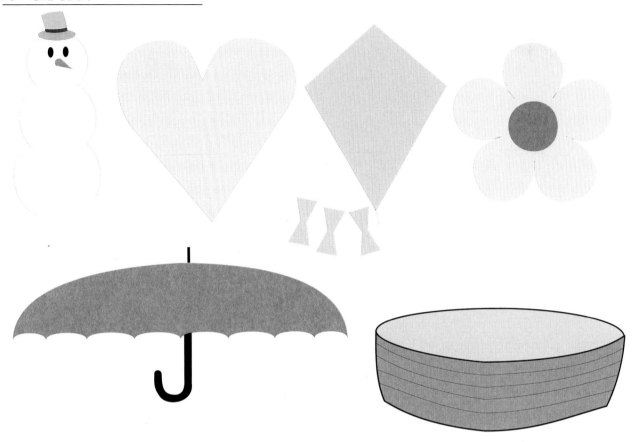

- Here are some shape ideas for each month:

January	snowman
February	heart
March	kite
April	umbrella
May	flower
June	boat
July	flag
August	berry
September	football
October	maple leaf
November	pumpkin
December	star

  What other shapes can you think of?

- Wrap a strip of masking tape around the yarn tip to act as a needle.

- Punch holes along the shape's edge. Weave the yarn in and out of the holes. Leave an opening at the top, and stuff the card with facial tissue to plump it out.

- Sew the card up with yarn, double wrap the last hole and slip the yarn tip in behind to secure the yarn.

- Write an appropriate message on the front of the card with markers or crayons, and decorate the card with stickers, glitter, and glue.

Discuss with your child the idea that you are using your hands to make gifts that will make people happy. In what other ways can we use our hands to make people happy? (Giving someone a hug or a friendly pat or writing someone a cheerful note are just a few ways we can use our hands for happiness.)

LET'S CHAT:

LOVABLE LOLLIPOPS

Lollipops make good gifts. But these lollipops will make great gifts! This is another project that several children can do at once. Make sure you have plenty of supplies to make lots of them!

THINGS YOU NEED:

Felt
Scissors
Craft glue
Wiggle eyes
Tracing paper

LET'S BEGIN:

- Trace the animal shapes onto tracing paper, and cut the pieces out. Use the pieces as patterns to cut two pieces of each shape.

- If you have more than one child with you, have each child cut a piece of felt.

- Place a little stream of glue around the top and sides of the animal.

*Cut two copies of each pattern.
Put a thick bead of glue around
the top and sides of the back piece
as shown.*

*Carefully place the front onto the back,
and press firmly where you have put the glue.*

- Glue the wiggle eyes on each animal's face. Cut and glue the nose and mouth from contrasting colors of felt.

- Place each cover over a lollipop.

- Lovable Lollipops also double as colorful puppets for extra entertainment!

LET'S CHAT:

If you're doing this project with older children, see if they can make lollipop covers that resemble the members of your family (see the See What I Did! project on page 97 for ideas). Can your child make up a play with the lollipop friends?

MAGNETIC PUZZLES

Imagine your preschooler's pride in bringing a handmade gift to the next birthday party! A Magnetic Puzzle is a wonderful gift idea for a preschool friend—if you can get your child to stop playing with it long enough to wrap it!

THINGS YOU NEED:

Construction paper

Magnet tape

Glue

Scissors

Old magazine pictures

Crayons or markers

Large envelope

LET'S BEGIN:

- Draw pictures on construction paper or cut out colorful magazine pictures.

- Glue the picture onto another piece of construction paper.

- Cut the picture into interesting-shaped jigsaw pieces.

Put two or three strips of magnet tape on the back of an envelope, and put your puzzle pieces inside.

PETER'S PERFECT PUZZLE PACKAGE

- Cut small pieces of magnet tape, and stick them onto the backs of the jigsaw pieces.

- Put the pieces on the refrigerator or another metal surface.

- Decorate a large envelope for storing the puzzle pieces. Cut and stick two or three small pieces of magnet tape on the back of the envelope. Place it on the refrigerator for easy access.

- You can make several Magnetic Puzzles and have contests to see how quickly you can put them together!

LET'S CHAT:

"A friend is a present that you give yourself." Discuss the meaning of this saying with your child. In what ways can you *be* a present to someone else?

HEART BASKET

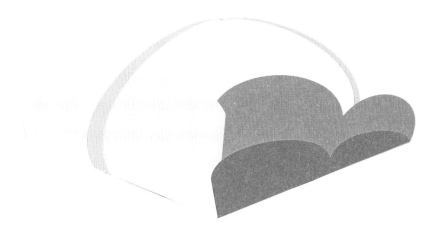

The Heart Basket is quick and easy to make. Younger children may need a little help to cut out the hearts and fit them together, but even they can make this pretty basket. Decorate the basket with heart stickers or other decorations to make it even prettier, and put in a few very lightweight gifts—some cut flowers, three or four cookies, a Lovable Lollipop (page 80), Cuplet Puppets (page 46), or Fuzzy Pencil Friends (page 76).

THINGS YOU NEED:

Construction paper

Glue

Scissors

Pencil

Tracing paper

Stickers or other decorations (optional)

Easter grass or confetti (optional)

LET'S BEGIN:

- Trace the heart pattern onto tracing paper and cut it out. Use this as a pattern to cut four hearts from construction paper. You can make the basket one color, two colors, or four colors.

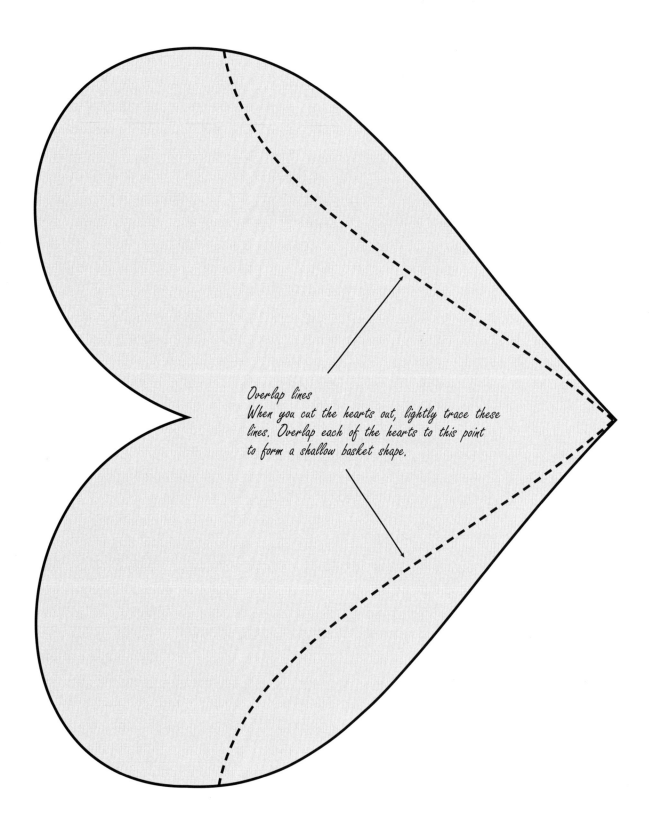

Overlap lines
When you cut the hearts out, lightly trace these
lines. Overlap each of the hearts to this point
to form a shallow basket shape.

Lay the four hearts flat, so the points are just touching. Overlap one heart over another, to the dashed line. Tape or glue the heart in place. Repeat this for all four hearts. Glue the handle in place, and you're done!

- Glue the hearts together to form a basket (see diagram).

- Cut a piece of construction paper 1½" by 12". Glue it to the basket as a handle.

- Decorate the basket and handle with stickers or other decorations.

- Fill the Heart Basket with Easter grass or confetti and a few lightweight goodies and . . . "Surprise!"

Children, as we all know, sometimes have a falling out, even with a best friend. Saying, "I'm sorry," and presenting a Heart Basket full of flowers or a package of sugarless bubblegum can help your child heal the hurt feelings. What are some other ways to show we are sorry for hurtful things we have said or done? Discuss with your child that forgiving one another and bearing with one another is a part of friendship and love.

LET'S CHAT:

WOVEN PAPER BASKET

Older children will enjoy the challenge of basket weaving. Younger children can help pick what three colors of construction paper you'll use and what will go in the basket when it's finished, but they may tire before the weaving is done. You might try the Heart Basket first, and then see if your child wants to tackle this.

The cardboard reinforced bottom allows this basket to carry a few heavier objects (such as dyed Easter eggs), but you'll want to fill it mostly with lighter gifts (Sponge Flowers, page 22; Fuzzy Pencil Friends, page 76; Lovable Lollipops, page 80; and so forth). Friends of ours made these as Easter baskets and filled them with lightweight toys and a few cookies and candies—the baskets held up for the backyard egg hunt and are still in use today.

You needn't wait until Easter to surprise someone with a Woven Paper Basket filled with goodies and fun. Whom can you treat with a happy-birthday basket, a get-well basket, a thank-you basket . . . ?

THINGS YOU NEED:

Three colors of construction paper
Cardboard or posterboard
Glue

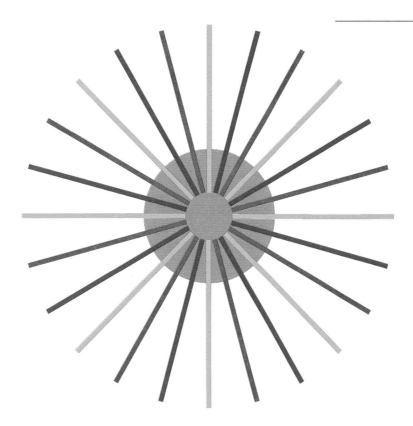

Scissors

Stapler

Straightedge

Pencil

Tape

Easter grass or confetti (optional)

LET'S BEGIN:

- You will need sixty strips of construction paper 1/4" wide by 9" long, but you don't want to spend all afternoon cutting paper strips! If you don't have access to a paper cutter, measure and cut a strip of cardboard 1/4" wide by 9" long. Use this as a guide for marking the construction paper for cutting.

- Place the cardboard guide flush with the left edge of one sheet of construction paper and lightly draw a pencil line down the right edge of the guide. Move the guide over and draw another pencil line. Repeat this until you have marked twenty strips on the construction paper.

- Now use the marked sheet of construction paper as a cutting guide and carefully cut through all three pieces of paper at once.

- Glue three construction paper strips of the same color together to make a strip ¼"wide by about 25" long. Make twelve strips, four of each of your three colors. Set them aside to let the glue dry.

- Copy the 7" diameter circle onto tracing paper. Cut the tracing paper, and use it as a pattern for cutting one circle from cardboard or posterboard and two circles from construction paper.

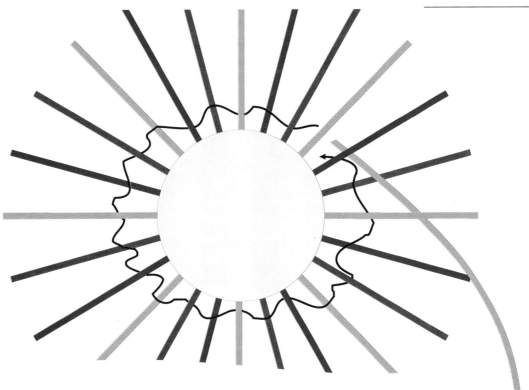

- Place the cardboard circle on the table and the glue the remaining twenty-four 1/4″ by 9″ strips of construction paper to the cardboard as shown. Remember to alternate colors.

- Cover the cardboard and the construction paper strips with one of the construction paper circles and glue the circle down. Glue the other construction paper circle to the other side of the cardboard circle.

- Cut two strips of construction paper 3″ wide by 12″ long and tape them to form a 7″ circle. Place this circle inside the basket. This makes the weaving easier because it gives you a guide to form the basket around.

- Now you are ready to weave. Take one 1/4″ by 25″ strip and, starting at the bottom of the basket, go over one vertical paper strip, under the next, and so on as shown until you have circled the basket. Overlap the ends of the strip until it fits snugly around the construction paper circle inside the basket; glue the overlapped ends together.

- Take a 1/4″ by 25″ strip of another color and begin weaving in and out just above the first woven strip. Where you went behind a vertical strip, now go in front of it, and vice versa. Overlap the ends and glue them as above. Then weave in your third color, overlap the ends, and glue them.

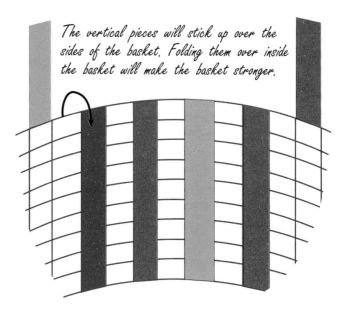

The vertical pieces will stick up over the sides of the basket. Folding them over inside the basket will make the basket stronger.

- Continue weaving, alternating colors, until you have used nine strips.

- Remove the inner circle of paper. Bend the vertical strips to the inside of the basket and glue them to the woven strips as shown. This helps keep the woven strips in place.

- Fit the inner circle of paper inside the basket again. This circle reinforces the sides of the basket; you want it to fit snugly against the woven sides. Adjust the size of the circle if you need to, and once the fit is right, glue the inner circle to the woven sides.

- Lay out the remaining three paper strips and glue them together on each end. Glue this to the inside of the basket as a handle. Hold the handle up for a few seconds to allow the glue to set.

- Cut three pieces of construction paper (of the same color) 3″ wide by 12″ long. Fold each piece in thirds and glue the last folded edge (see diagram).

- Reinforce the handles using the folded construction paper strips. Place one folded strip on each side on the handle, pushing the paper to the bottom of the basket. Staple through the handle, the reinforcement, and the basket side near the top of the basket. Glue the bottom of the handle reinforcement to the side of the basket.

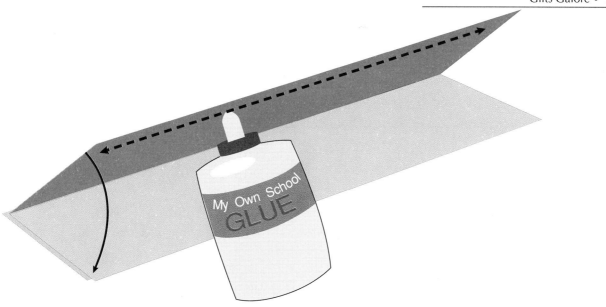

- Place the remaining piece of reinforcement at the top of the handle so that it overlaps the other reinforcing pieces and fits the handle snugly. Staple this piece to the other two, stapling through the handle and the reinforcement.

- Fill the basket with Easter grass and goodies, and your gift is ready!

Basket weaving is an ancient art. American Indians wove baskets so tightly that they could carry water in them! A beautiful, well-woven basket can become an expensive collector's item. Do you live near any places where basket weaving is still done today? Why not visit the library together and find out more about basket weaving?

LET'S CHAT:

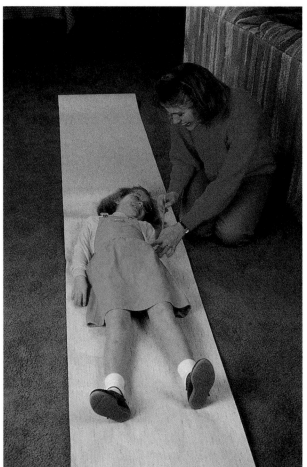

I'M GLAD
THAT I'M ME!

Our children are confronted by thousands of advertising images each day. Be cool! Be hip! Be rad! As a result, most of our children become convinced that they're not cool, hip, or rad (whatever that is)—and that life cannot continue unless they instantly *become* cool, hip, and rad. They receive many of the same messages from peers at school. How many times have you fought with your child over whether he can be seen in school with a certain pair of pants? Simply put, if we send our children out in the world searching for an identity, there are lots of people willing to provide one—or sell one.

The solution is to provide your child with an identity all his very own. Stress to your child that he is the most important person in the world. He doesn't have to be just like everyone else—in fact, to quote Mr. Rogers, "There's nobody else quite like you."

The projects in this section all revolve around the idea of encouraging your child to be proud of who he or she is. Whether the project is mounting a Life Line on the wall or putting together "See What I Did!" Clothespins, use the projects in this section as the medium for encouraging your child to be proud of himself.

All of the projects in this section can be made by children of any age. Parents will have to be more involved with the Life Line and the Self-Portrait (you're taller, and your child should not be working on a ladder), but each of these projects was designed to interest a wide range of youngsters.

Encourage your child to make choices and decisions—which color paper should we use? Which picture should we put on the magnet? Which pair of pants should we put in the Self-Portrait? As you work, praise your child for being so helpful. The nurturing support you give to your child now will make a world of difference in the years ahead.

PICTURE MAGNET

A picture magnet will be a wonderful addition to your refrigerator! These are so useful that you should make three or four and have one for every member of the family!

THINGS YOU NEED:

Assorted lids

Magnet tape

Scissors

Pencil

Child's photo

Glue

Construction paper

LET'S BEGIN:

- Place your child's photograph on the table, face up. Place a lid on the photograph, making sure that the lid completely covers the face. Trace around the lid with a pencil.

- Cut the photo out on the traced line with scissors.

- Spread glue over the inside of the lid, as shown. Place the photo on the lid and let the glue dry.

- Cut a small strip of magnet tape. Turn the lid upside down and press the magnet tape on.

- Once you've done a few, try cutting a design from construction paper for additional decoration. Cut a circle from construction paper and glue it on the lid—then glue the photo onto the construction paper. You can also add ribbon bows, lace, etc. for more decoration.

What pictures does your child like best? If you're using construction paper or other decoration, talk about why the color of the decoration matches (or doesn't match!) the colors in the photo. Does your child have, um, unconventional tastes? Celebrate! It's important to encourage your child, even if the colors clash.

LET'S CHAT:

"SEE WHAT I DID!" CLOTHESPIN

Along the same vein as the photo magnet is the "See What I Did!" clothespin. Use it to display pictures, awards, homework, or report cards. It also is a clever gift idea for decorating the refrigerator door of a doting grandparent.

THINGS YOU NEED:

Spring-type clothespin

Glue

Felt or construction paper

Cardstock or posterboard

Markers

Scissors

Wiggle eyes (optional)

Magnet tape

Tracing paper

LET'S BEGIN:

• Copy the patterns onto tracing paper. Cut out the pieces and use them as patterns to cut a head and two hands from felt or construction paper.

• Draw your child's facial features and hair on the paper face. For a felt face, cut a nose, a mouth, and hair out of other colors of felt and glue them on. Glue on the wiggle eyes and let the glue dry.

See What I Did!

- Write either "_____'s Work" or "See What I Did!" on a small rectangular piece of cardstock or posterboard. Glue all of the pieces to the clothespin.

LET'S CHAT:

As you work, talk about good character traits. Why should your child be proud of what she's done? At the same time, it might be a good idea to talk about the difference between being proud and being conceited.

"I AM SPECIAL" SCRAPBOOK

This scrapbook is special because it will hold a storehouse of memories, treasures, original thoughts, photographs, writings, and drawings. You and your child will cherish it for years!

THINGS YOU NEED:

Two pieces of posterboard or cardboard cut to 8½" by 11" or 11" by 14"

Paper punch

Two or three large metal rings, heavy yarn, or string leather

Construction paper

Lined notebook paper

Markers, crayons

Decorations—stickers, stars, cut-out shapes

Clear contact paper

LET'S BEGIN:

- Punch two or three holes in the book cover pieces either along the left edge or across the top. Hint: use three-holed paper as a guide to punch the holes.

- Punch the paper you'll use for the inside.

- Insert the paper between the book covers.

- Bind the covers and the inside with metal rings, yarn, or string leather.

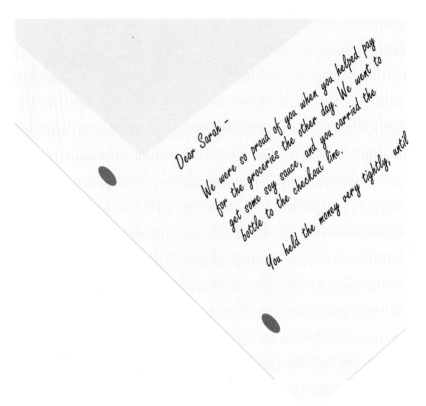

Dear Sarah –

We were so proud of you when you helped pay for the groceries the other day. We went to get some soy sauce, and you carried the bottle to the checkout line.

You held the money very tightly, until

- Help your child write his name on the cover. Guide his hand or draw a dot-to-dot for him to trace.

- Help your child decorate his bookcover. Use stars, stickers, cut-out shapes, family photos, magazine pictures, leaves, flowers, or other items.

- Cover the bookcovers with clear contact paper for preservation.

LET'S CHAT:

Use the scrapbook for holding special pictures, photographs, stories, poems, writings, trip souvenirs, awards—whatever is meaningful to your child. Record the dates of outings, birthdays, vacations, holidays, or special events and write the child's comments and reactions. Ask, "What did you like best and why?" or, "Describe the day. I'll be the secretary and write down what you say." (This will really make your child feel important and creates a lasting memory.)

Each year at the same time, take a photograph of your child for the book; underneath it write your child a letter. In the letter comment on his progress over the past year. What can he do now that he couldn't do last year at this time? Compliment him on acts of kindness and signs of character growth. Write, "I was really proud of you when you . . ."

ME TREE

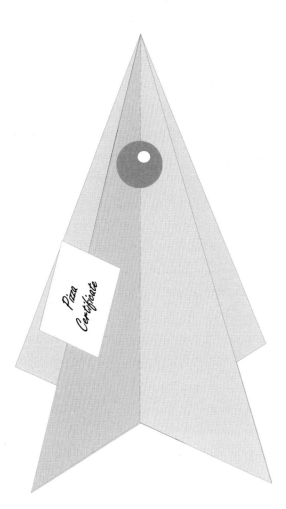

Make this special tree with your child, and place it in his room. The tree is made from corrugated cardboard to last a long time, so that you can change the decorations to match the seasons. (You might look at the Laced Cards project on page 77 for ideas.)

Children sometimes alternate between feeling that "there's nothing special about me" and being certain that "I'm the only person in the whole world with my problems." This tree is an excellent way to stress your child's unique characteristics and to emphasize your love for him.

You'll need a utility knife to properly cut the corrugated cardboard. Do not try to cut the cardboard without a metal ruler or straightedge as a cutting guide. Corrugated cardboard is tough, and you need the straightedge to protect yourself from serious cuts. As always, do NOT let your child handle the knife.

THINGS YOU NEED:

Corrugated cardboard

Green contact paper

Utility knife

Metal straightedge

Scissors

Construction paper

Tracing paper

Pencil

Paper punch

Yarn

LET'S BEGIN:

- Trace the tree patterns onto tracing paper. Cut the pieces out, and use them as patterns to mark the cardboard. Place the cardboard down on a workbench or other work surface, and cut the parts out with a utility knife and a metal straightedge. Note that we've included two patterns: you will need one copy of each pattern (slit-up and slit-down) in order to assemble a tree.

- Cover the pieces with green contact paper, making sure to keep the slits in the tree pieces open.

- Cut small slits in the edges of the tree (shown on the patterns) with the utility knife.

- Assemble the tree by sliding the two parts together. If the cardboard binds, don't force it. Take the pieces back to the workbench, and widen the slits with the utility knife and metal straightedge. (Safety tip: resist the temptation to "shave" the cardboard slit with your knife—put it down on a workbench and trim it with the straightedge.)

- Now you're ready to decorate the tree. Here are some suggestions:

  Hang items depicting your child's favorite interests such as baseball or football cards, paper dolls, or hair bows. Hang photos of favorite people on branches.

  Cut several leaf or fruit shapes from construction paper and decorate the tree for your child with notes, "I love you because . . ."

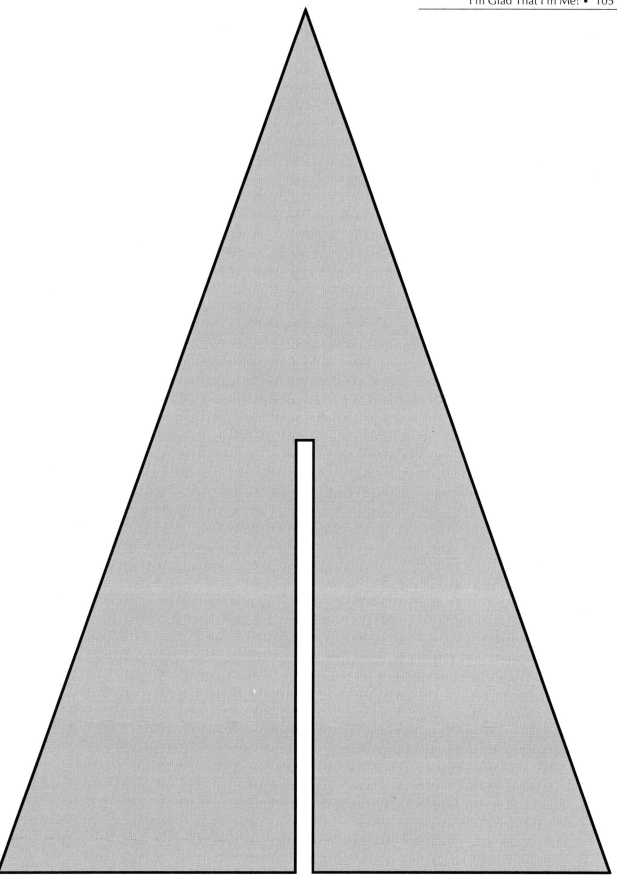

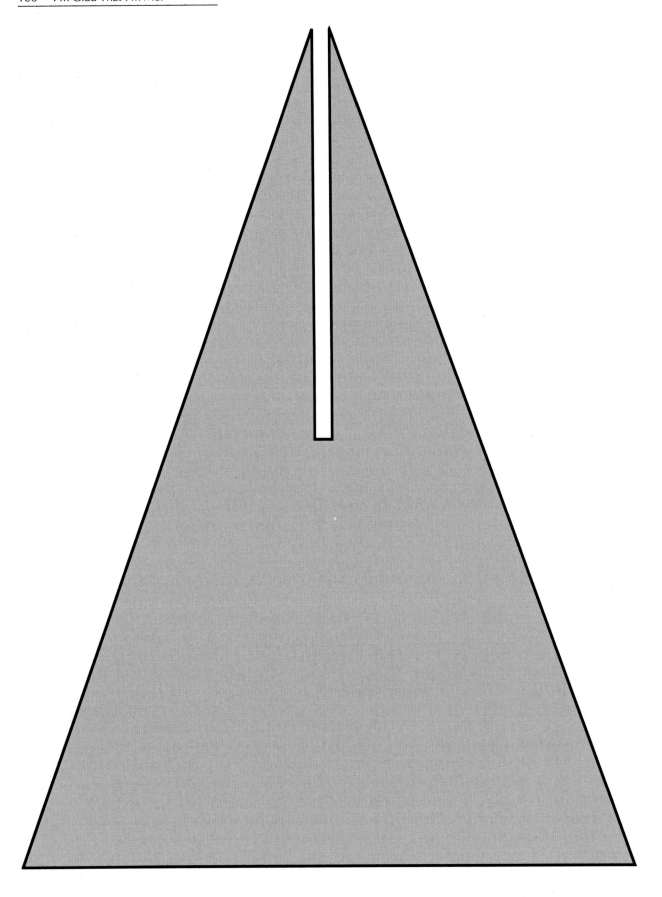

Decorate the tree seasonally—snowmen in winter, hearts in February, suns in summer, flowers in spring, or pumpkins in autumn.

Write promissory notes for an ice-cream cone jaunt, a nature hike, a pizza dinner, or a trip to the park or library. Your child can choose one each week!

Use tissue paper to decorate the "Me Tree" with blossoms. It will brighten up your home on rainy days!

Snuggle up and read "The Fir Tree" by Hans Christian Andersen to your child. Reading is a wonderful rainy day as well as "any day" activity.

LET'S CHAT:

V.I. P. MEDAL

Has she learned to tie her shoes? Has he finally made his bed by himself? Do you think your child deserves a medal? A V.I.P. Medal is for a Very Important Person—your child! Make a special event out of making the medal, to celebrate a special accomplishment.

THINGS YOU NEED:

Scissors

Construction paper or posterboard

Markers

Paper punch

24″ strand of yarn

Gummed stars

Pencil

Tracing paper

Small photographs of your child

Aluminum foil

White glue

Tape

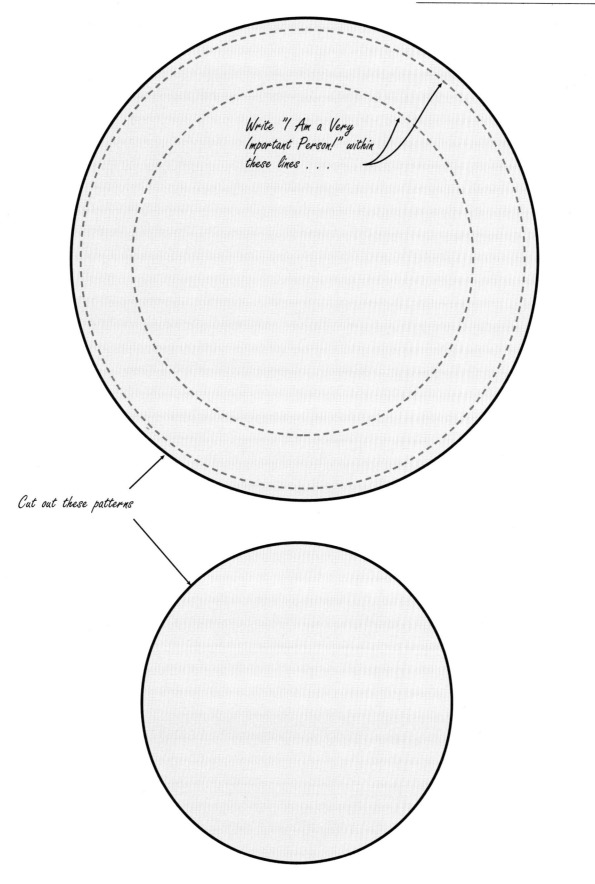

Write "I Am a Very Important Person!" within these lines . . .

Cut out these patterns

LET'S BEGIN:

- Copy the patterns onto tracing paper. Cut them out, and use them as patterns for cutting construction paper or posterboard.

- Cover the smaller circle with aluminum foil. Glue the smaller circle in the center of the larger one.

- Glue your child's photo in the center of the smaller circle, and letter your child's name around the outside of the larger circle. Decorate the medal with stars.

- Punch a hole in the top of the badge, and insert the yarn through the hole. You'll find the yarn easier to insert if a small piece of tape is wrapped around the tip. Now tie the ends together to make a long necklace with a medallion.

- Slip the V.I.P. Medal around your honoree's neck accompanied by a big hug!

LET'S CHAT:

How do we honor people? How do we show people respect? Tying her shoes or helping to pick up shows respect for Mom or Dad. What other ways can your child give honor to others?

LIFE LINE

Did your parents have a doorway where your height was measured each year? That special doorway with the faded paint is
one of the things that makes a house into a home. Nowadays,
though, the "typical" family moves every five years—this project lets you take that special doorway along with you when
you go.

THINGS YOU NEED:

A single roll of plain *strippable* wallpaper

Wallpaper sizing

Paint roller and tray, or paint brush

Straightedge

Wallpaper brush (optional)

Sponge

Utility knife

Ladder

Pencil

Measuring tape

Cloth measuring tape (this will become part of your Life Line)

Items that represent events or stages of your child's life—toys,
photographs, etc.

Construction paper

Crayons, markers

←— 21" —→

Measure the width of one roll. Mark that width on the wall in two locations.

Then, using a T-square, measure a vertical line on the wall.

Hang the wallpaper from this line – don't try to snug it up against the door. The door may not be precisely vertical . . .

Adhesive picture hangers (optional)

Monofilament fishing line (optional)

Glue or double-sided tape

LET'S BEGIN:

- Select a very good quality wallpaper—you will want to take it off the wall in one piece if you ever have to move. We recommend one of the heavy vinyl papers. *Be sure to keep the manufacturer's instructions for stripping your wallpaper.*

- Carefully measure and mark a line on the wall in your home or apartment where you want to put up the Life Line; locating it beside a doorway or corner makes your measuring easier. If you have more than one child, consider a location near their room(s).

- *Before hanging the wallpaper, treat the wall area with wallpaper sizing according the directions on the package—this will make stripping the wallpaper later much easier.*

- Follow the manufacturer's instructions for putting up the wallpaper. Instructions vary from brand to brand, but don't worry, they're all pretty easy.

Joan   Sarah   *Joan   Sarah*

6

5

4   4

3   3

2   2

1   1

Mount the wallpaper, and place the cloth measuring tape in the center. If you have more than one child, create a space for each.

Cut out large numbers and use them to show your child's size at different ages.

Make your Life Line extra special by hanging up your child's favorite baby and toddler toys.

Adhesive picture hangers work very well. Tie a loop of monofilament fishing line around the object, and hang it up!

- You may want to let the wallpaper dry on the wall for a few hours before you put on any heavy toys. Once the paper is on the wall securely, mount the measuring tape. If the wallpaper doesn't have a vertical stripe in it, you might want to make a very light mark with a pencil. Have your child hold the end of the tape right at the floor. Make sure that she realizes which side of the tape should be face-out! Starting from the bottom, apply a very small bead of glue to the back of the tape, and press it against the wall as you go up. Be very careful to keep the tape straight along your line. (You can also use double-sided tape to achieve the same thing.)

- Cut out large numerals, one through ten, and space them along the Life Line. The numerals will give your child a perspective of the passage of time as you insert items and photographs.

- Look through photograph albums together; choose one or two infant pictures and attach them at the line's beginning before numeral one. Choose a rattle, teething toy, or other early favorite plaything and mount it with double-sided tape.

- Be sure to include a picture or drawing of all the places she has lived.

- Remember that a photograph or drawing of each family member is important.

- Write the date or year of each event on drawings and photographs.

- Attach stuffed animals and toys to represent favorites at different ages. If the toy has a loop or something similar on the back, hang it on an adhesive picture hook. If there isn't a loop, tie a loop of monofilament fishing line around the toy and loop it over the picture hook. The fishing line will be invisible once it's on the wall.

- Lest we forget: have your child stand against the measuring tape, and strike a line to show her height. Write the date you measured her next to the mark.

Even though you'll undoubtedly know more of the events than your child will, encourage her to think of what things should go on the Life Line. Ask questions and make suggestions to fill in the blanks. You'll be surprised at how many things your child remembers.

LET'S CHAT:

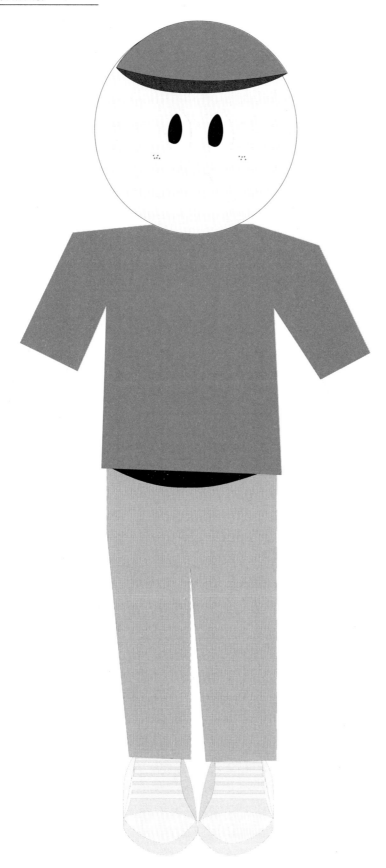

SELF-PORTRAIT

What do I look like? How do others see me? What an opportunity for discussing and stressing your child's exceptional characteristics! In this project you and your child will spend a couple of hours creating a self-portrait. Not a painting, but a three-dimensional wall hanging!

THINGS YOU NEED:

A single roll of plain *strippable* wallpaper

Wallpaper sizing (optional)

Paint roller and tray, or paint brush

Wallpaper brush (optional)

Old or worn clothes

An old hat

A worn out pair of sneakers

Pencil and crayons

Straightedge

Scissors

Seam ripper

Measuring tape

Large sponge

Pump sprayer (optional)

Utility knife

Ladder

LET'S BEGIN:

• Unroll the wallpaper on the floor, with the finished side up. Have your child lie down on the paper, with his feet at the end of the roll. Trace lightly around the youngster with a pencil or crayon.

• Carefully measure a vertical line where you'll place the wallpaper. A doorway or corner makes an excellent location.

• Carefully measure the height of the wall where you'll hang the finished portrait. Mark off the distance on the wallpaper, measuring from the bottom of the child's drawn feet. Remember to leave an inch or so on the top to ensure that the wallpaper fits; you'll cut off the extra at the top with a utility knife and straightedge once you have hung the wallpaper.

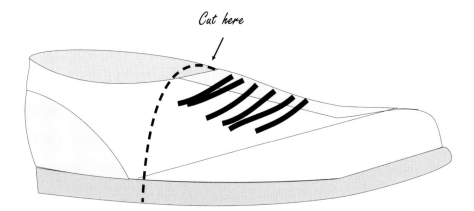

- If you keep old clothes someplace, now's the time to bring them out. What were his favorite pants? His favorite shirt? Select a pair of pants and a shirt (pants that have worn through in the seat are perfect). You should also pick out two samples from your collection of orphan socks.

- Using a seam ripper or a pair of scissors, rip out the seams along the legs of the pants and the sides of the shirt.

- Use a stout pair of scissors or (ideally) a pair of tin snips to cut the sneakers in half crossways at the top of the laces. Similarly, cut the cap or hat in half crossways at the crown, and cut the socks off at the heel.

- Glue the tops of the socks into place, lining up the heel of each sock with the bottom of the feet on the paper. Then make a quick stitch or two through the paper to anchor the socks in place.

- Attach the pants next. Pay careful attention to how far down the pants come over the socks—you'll want to leave room for the sneakers. Does your child tuck in his shirt? If he usually does, wait until after the next step to tack down the top of the pants.

- Attach the shirt to the wallpaper. As above, glue the piece down and use a few stitches at each corner. If you just

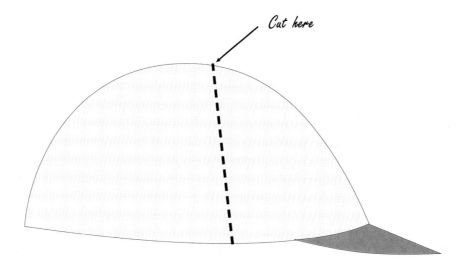

Cut here

glue and stitch at the corners, the shirt will "drape" properly once it's mounted on the wall.

- Attach the sneakers to the wallpaper by making a series of stitches through the tongue of the sneaker into the wallpaper. All you want to do with the stitch is keep the sneaker attached to the wallpaper—the sneakers will sit on the floor when you have the project finished.

- Place a piece of masking tape or other sturdy adhesive tape along the back of the cap. Tape it to the top of the drawing. Now fold the cap back, and color in the face, neck, and hands.

- Color the portrait with crayons or markers. Draw in facial features, fingernails, hair, and clothing.

- Gently, carefully, turn the whole project upside down, so that the glued side of the wallpaper is showing. Be careful with the sneakers!

- We recommend that you treat the wall area with wallpaper sizing before hanging the wallpaper. The wallpaper will hang more easily and will also be easier to remove when your child (by then college age!) has tired of his Self-Portrait. Just follow the directions on the sizing package.

← 21" →

Measure the width of one roll. Mark that width on the wall in two locations.

Then, using a T-square, measure a vertical line on the wall.

Hang the wallpaper from this line — don't try to snug it up against the door. The door may not be precisely vertical . . .

- Using a pump sprayer or a soaking wet sponge, wet the back of the wallpaper. The directions probably call for soaking the entire piece in a tray, but spraying will work. Some wallpapers must "book" after you've soaked them: Double the paper over and join the top and bottom ends of the piece together, and let it sit for a few minutes. Check the instructions that came with your wallpaper for details; some wallpapers go up immediately while others book for several minutes.

- Now, carefully hang the project on the wall. Smooth out the wrinkles with a damp sponge. Cut off any excess wallpaper at the top, using a straightedge and a utility knife.

- Once the project is mounted on the wall, you might want to use a strong adhesive to glue the sneakers to the wallpaper (to prevent them being kicked off by passing feet).

LET'S CHAT:

Much of our self-esteem depends on how we see ourselves. Does your child like the picture? Does he like who he sees? Be sure to stress that height, weight, and hair color aren't important—what is important is recognizing that God made your child to be very special.

INDEX

About this book:

Rainy Day Projects for Children was typeset using a digital rendition of Herman Zapf's classic *Optima*. The type was set on a Linotype Linotronic 300 by Desktop Dynamics of Lakewood, New Jersey. Illustrations were generated electronically and produced on the Linotronic. Photographs were separated and stripped electronically on the ColorPage II system at Spectrum, Inc. in Golden, Colorado.

Text stock for the book is 70 pound Finch Fine VHF, an uncoated supercalendared sheet that permits the reader to make notes in pencil and wipe the smudges of small children; it permits the publisher to print very fine resolution pictures and illustrations. It is made by Finch, Pruyn & Company of Glens Falls, New York. The book was printed and bound by R. R. Donnelley & Sons Company in Willard, Ohio.